Empire on the Verge of a Nervous Breakdown

Empire on
the Verge of a
Nervous Breakdown

MARY S. GOSSY

LIVERPOOL UNIVERSITY PRESS

First published 2009 by
Liverpool University Press
4 Cambridge Street
Liverpool
L69 7ZU

British Library Cataloguing-in-Publication data
A British Library CIP record is available

ISBN 978-1-84631-182-6

Typeset in Borges by
Koinonia, Manchester
Printed in Great Britain by the
MPG Books Group, Bodmin and King' Lynn

Contents

Acknowledgements

With thanks to the very many people who have loved and encouraged me over the years of reading and writing it took to make this little manuscript, especially my father. Thanks, Mom. Thanks to the women of Friday night at Moonstruck Diner, to Myra K., Lisa D., Mikey, Anny, Steve, and Paulie. Thanks to the nuns at Fairacres. Thanks to Gayle, Christy, Suzanne, Lewis and Clark, the monks at 980 and Emery House. Thanks to Eileen, Terry, Gillian, and the nuns at Freeland, the friars at Mt. Sinai and St. Elizabeth's. Thank you, Marcia. Thanks to the whole holy community at Women's and Gender Studies at Rutgers: Wisdom hath built herself a house there, and may it stand strong. Paul Julian Smith, thank you. Thanks to my students from the Spring term of 2007, especially the group in the Audre Lorde class. Thank you to Anthony Cond and all at Liverpool University Press for their creativity, help and support of this project.

Thank you to all, names known and unknown, who have shared your love over these years, daring over the differences to open and give and receive again and again.

Mary Gossy
Oxford, 2007
The Bronx, 2008

CHAPTER ONE

Verging On

Losing power is scary. Being on the verge of a breakdown of domination and control produces panic attacks. These essays form a collection of case studies of symptoms and attempts at adaptation or writing-through produced in texts that appear in critical moments of literary or political history, moments in which imperial projects show signs of insupportable stress. They are literary texts, because literature presents the multivalent charges of cultural anxiety as "a mode of cultural work, the work of giving-to-read those impossible contradictions that cannot yet be spoken."[1] Literature gives access to the "verge," to the place where the full terror of falling is felt, and yet both feet are still on the ground.

In these essays the reader will meet verges of cliffs, madness, window ledges, rooftops; verges of virgins and whores, slippery slopes and razors' edges. The allusion to Pedro Almódovar's 1988 film *Women on the Verge of a Nervous Breakdown* (*Mujeres al borde de un ataque de nervios*) is meant to invoke the symptoms manifested by the texts under discussion. In these cases non-Spanish writers are on the edge and very jumpy, and their nervousness reveals itself in strong and complicated allusions to Spain. The texts of James Joyce, Gertrude Stein, A. Conan Doyle, Edgar Allan Poe, Sigmund Freud and his patient the Wolf-Man, Al Jolson, and Billie Holiday are very nervous around gender, and in particular around strange femininities, and the idea of Spain makes them more than twitchy. To the extent that "women" are on the verge of a "nervous" breakdown, so is empire, in these texts, on the verge of a Spanish breakdown. "Women" and "empire," "nervous" and "Spanish" commingle in each other's connotative fields. In these texts masculinity and femininity are always on the verge of slipping away from what they are supposed to be, and of dragging fantasies of imperial domination over the edge with them. The Spain of lost empire accompanies these acute symptoms of anxiety, even in texts and authors where—as in Monty Python's version of the Spanish Inquisition—no one expects it. For both a European and a U.S. imagination, Spain is always on the verge. Since 711 (we might insist on saying 7/11, such is the anxiety provoked by this moment in the minds of non-Muslim medieval Europeans) when North African Muslims conquered the Iberian peninsula, Spain has been the location of difference in Europe, whether that difference is feared (as Muslim), desired (as ruined, Romantic, Gypsy), or envied (as dominant world power, from 1492 through the so-called Golden Age). People may know nothing of the Moors, and the collapse of the Roman Empire may seem, to some, to be very far away, but the after-shocks of the fall of Spain resonate everywhere, along with persistent echoes of denial. Big U.S.-manufactured automobiles named Granada, Seville, Cordoba, and Eldorado are rusting away in plain sight all over the landscape, reminders of the fragility and obsolescence of conquest and reconquest as ways of being in the world. A U.S. President who is fluent in neither English nor Spanish insisted throughout his recent term on making unintelligible pronouncements in both languages, ultimately with far-reaching political consequences, particularly in relation to borders and the immigration of Spanish-speaking Americans.

When empire is on the verge of a Spanish breakdown, gender and historical anxiety hysterically affect textuality. So the texts read here represent the full-blown symptoms of empire on the verge. They provide vivid demonstrations of imperial anxiety in action. The readings work through the symptoms of power panic by articulating love and trauma through rhetorics and thematics that plunge over the verge directly into the breach, admitting the possibility of being wounded, living through being wounded, and then writing from being wounded, in a condition in which the inability to heal (to erase the effects and memory of being wounded) makes a healing way of telling stories possible. As a group these essays flow into each other, with an inexorable reiteration of the themes of power, love, the erotic, the unconscious, the wound, healing, difference, writing, and reading. They are about writing and reading and the relationship of those two practices to political and social life.

In each case the texts read here are narratives. Some are explicitly prose narratives, some slip from prose toward poetry or move across genres from lyric to epic, from poetry to prose. Yet each text tells a story with an explicitly historical aim. In this respect, these narratives participate in the double-meanings inherent in the Spanish word "historia." "Historia" means both "history," the written record of the past, and simply "story," like the ones you may have heard late at night from a parental narrator at your bedside. In Spanish, "history" is always a "story," and a "story" is always "history." The narrative impulse is an archival impulse as well as a creative or innovative one. To the extent that subjectivity is invented in storytelling, narrative is a crucial genre. Historically, it has tended to require the blood sacrifice of female or feminized bodies in order to propagate itself. Rare indeed is the canonical narrative that does not kill a woman or some feminized being. And yet, of course, there are exceptions, and the novel at the root of modern Western narrative, Cervantes's *Don*

Quijote, is one of them. Cervantes's work is a constant intertextual presence in the writings under discussion. This book concludes with an essay on reading, writing, and the *Quijote*. In this text, women, nervous breakdowns, empires, and Spain come into history by way of the pen of a writer with a war-wound that does not heal. An effect of this is not that the pen is mightier than the sword, but the realization that the pen is different from the sword, that writing and reading, like living, need not be a question of killing or being killed. These texts show that to be a subject is to be wounded. Breakdowns of empire, sexuality, and power affect whether or not, and how and why the story of the wound is told, and whether or not, or how or why the disabling wound itself enables narrative. All this may not require killing or being killed, but it is a matter of life and death.

Note

1 Barbara Johnson, "Introduction," *The Feminist Difference: Literature, Psychoanalysis, Race, and Gender* (Cambridge, MA: Harvard University Press, 1998), 13.

CHAPTER TWO

The End

[T]he Spanish girls laughing in their shawls and their tall combs and the auctions in the morning the Greeks and the jews and the Arabs and the devil knows who else from all the ends of Europe.[1]

The last pages of James Joyce's *Ulysses* provide the reader with a jumping-off point for the study of imperial anxiety. In this case, the plank that empire must walk is Gibraltar. That rock marks the end of empire, in the sense that it was the *ne plus ultra* of Roman domination of the Mediterranean, *Mare Nostrum*, Our Sea. It also marks the beginning of empire, in that it is the gateway through which a New World, what would come to be called the Americas, was colonized. In the United States, Gibraltar became an emblem of mid-twentieth-century North American economic solidity and power. For generations, the Prudential Insurance Company invited Americans to "own a piece of the Rock." American power too, invested its self-idealization in that chunk of real estate at the end and beginning of empire.

Gibraltar marks a confluence of oppositions around imperial ambition and anxiety. To begin with, it is the end. It is the end of the world, in a psychically catastrophic as well as a geographic sense. It marks the point of no return. Edward Gibbon begins and ends his geographical survey of the classical world at the *start* of *Decline and Fall of the Roman Empire* with the Rock of Gibraltar; his title declares that he, too, is beginning with the end; the name of the book is not "History of...," "Birth of...," "Trajectory of..." the Roman Empire. It is *Decline and Fall*. Gibbon begins his story of the end at the end of the earth. The nation he finds here is Spain, the old imperial nemesis of Gibbon's England. Although he loved Great Britain's empire no more than he loved Rome's, there are nevertheless hints of a rivalry with Spain in some of his sentences.[2] And no wonder: Gibraltar is a prismatic hall of imperial mirrors. From one angle the observer can see in it Rome's beginning and fall; from another the glittering opening and nebulous collapse of the Spanish empire; from yet another the teetering preciousness of a Union Jack holding sway over only a few square miles of precipitous cliffs. Underlying the whole series of holographic apparitions is the name itself, Gebel al Tarik, or "Tarik's Mountain," with its invocation of Muslim conquest, simultaneously past, present, and future. What Gibraltar's intransigent permanence marks and insists on is what imperial ambition never wants to admit: empire has failure built into it.

Gibraltar is Moorish, Spanish, Christian, French, English, Muslim, Irish, Roman, and more: "the devil knows who else from all the ends of Europe." Molly Bloom helps to enunciate the unknowable difference that always eludes the fist of empire. To say "the devil knows" is also to say no one knows. The ends of Europe are not neatly tied up. The ends of empire are loose, too; something is always slipping by. The greater the effort to limit, to name, to control, even to exterminate difference, the more apparent it becomes that some little bit of difference will always slide away. For James Joyce and Edward Gibbon, as well as for Edgar Allan Poe, Sigmund Freud, Monique Wittig, and the anonymous author of the *Celestina*, for the Wolf-Man and Al Jolson and even for Monty Python and Gertrude Stein, this slippery difference tends to appear when a text symptomatically invokes Spain.

Spain is for western Europeans and for North Americans the symptom par excellence of empire lost and found. It is a territory and an idea physically and metaphorically at the end of the world. It is the place where Islam penetrated the West most deeply and lastingly. As such, it is a locus of anxiety about femininity and passivity, of persistent doubt about paternity and masculinity. Diderot said that "Africa begins at the Pyrenees," enshrining racism and cultural triumphalism at once. But what is obvious in his famous remark is, in fact, a negation of rock-solid reality. Spain is part of Europe. There are Muslims in France. Mountain ranges are full of passes. Insistent efforts to delineate once and for all the boundaries of difference never reach their goal. To the extent that empire's goal is to make you work for me, I must define you as strictly separate from and unlike me. But the uncanny is always at work in these operations, and so I must make what is most like me most unlike me in order to proceed with my imperial project. Diderot can say of Spain, which shares a very long border with France, "Africa (not me) begins there (very, very close to me). Further, I have no idea what Africa is. I do have some idea what Spain is, though, and so I will say that Spain is Africa." In the logic of empire, what is near is far, what is familiar is unfamiliar, what is powerful is weak. Imperial thinking is structured by irrational oppositions and inversions. Empire fears what is not dangerous, and ignores real threats. (In the present day, it is destroyed by homemade devices, yet obsessed by non-existent weapons of mass destruction.[3])

Spain is in this cultural context a menacing symptom not only of racial and ethnic difference, but also of sexual difference. It marks the place where empire is vulnerable to sexual intimidation, or where it seeks forbidden gratifications. In these and other respects the idea of Spain has something in common with other places and peoples which have been subjected to orientalizing discourses and ideations. But the specificity of Spain is its nearness to, indeed its physical membership, in the body of empire. It is different and the same at once, and thus has a unique capacity, however unlucky, for bearing the symptomatic burdens of Euro-American empires. It is not a coincidence that the reader should find, in Joyce's *Ulysses*, "a text which imaginatively superimposes the Mediterranean basin upon Dublin."[4] According to Elizabeth Butler Cullingford,

> The Moorish–Iberian–Irish connection evoked during Molly's reminiscences of Gibraltar is historical rather than mythic. Yeats's great-grandfather, "trading out of Galway into Spain," and his great-grandfather, the "Old merchant skipper who leaped overboard / After a ragged hat in Biscay Bay" (*Collected Poems*, 101), were following an ancient shipping route memorialized today by the Spanish Arch of the quays of Galway.[5]

The Bay of Biscay is nowhere near Gibraltar, but it is entirely likely that sailors traveled back and forth along the edge of the world from Spain to Ireland and back again. And of course there is the tremendous irony that Philip the Second's Armada was wrecked off the Irish coast, making of that island the bridge over which dominion passed finally from Spain to England. An Irish–Spanish connection seems indubitable. The final, emphatic section of *Ulysses* insists on the specificity of Gibraltar—end and beginning, Spanish and British, Christian and Muslim—as the headland and terminus of difference.

Gibraltar is where Molly gives up her virginity. It could rightly be said to be the birthplace of *Ulysses*. If that text superimposes the Mediterranean basin upon Dublin, it can also be said to make of Gibraltar and Molly a hypertext of body and rock. Gibraltar is for Molly a home that is no more, a place of loss and gain, of coincidences of familiarity and strangeness. In some respects, it is a geographical and historical consolidation of the uncanny, and that makes it even more specifically allied to Molly's body. For Freud, uncanny sensations arise when the familiar and the strange collide in a process of remembering and repression that goes back to our earliest symbolic experiences. Specifically, the uncanny refers always to the female genitals, simultaneously the homiest and the most foreign place of them all:

> It often happens that neurotic men declare that they feel there is something uncanny about the female genital organs. This *unheimlich* place, however, is the entrance to the former *Heim* [home] of all human beings, to the place where each one of us lived once upon a time and in the beginning. There is a joking saying that "Love is home-sickness"; and whenever a man dreams of a place or a country and says to himself, while he is still dreaming: "this place is familiar to me, I've been here before," we may interpret the place as being his mother's genitals or her body. In this case too, then, the *unheimlich* is what was once *heimisch*, familiar; the prefix "*un*" ["un"] is the token of repression.[6]

In the course of the "Penelope" chapter, Molly urinates, defecates, menstruates, and masturbates. Her genitalia rise up from passivity to perform a percussive backbeat to the verbal run of her thoughts. Her body and her language are inseparable.[7] In this respect, she shows a compelling divergence from an imperial textualizing that depends upon repression and an unconscious rhetoric rigidified by formulaic fantasies of omnipotence.

The rhetoric of empire is irrevocably split from the bodies of imperialists. It does not say what it means, because it cannot feel anything; it feels only through the mediated sensations of the bodies it subjugates. An example of this may be found in Gibbon. Gibbon may have hated empires, but his writing about them is imperial. At the conclusion of *Decline and Fall* he says:

> It was among the ruins of the Capitol that I first conceived the idea of a work which has amused and exercised near twenty years of my life, and which, however inadequate to my own wishes, I finally deliver to the curiosity and candour of the public. (3.880)

One of the first efforts of empire is to take over the fruits of the labor of the colonized. It does this by "working over" the bodies of the colonized. Of course, this comes at the price of alienation from the imperialist's own body. Once an imperial system is in place, the price of power is disembodiment, feeling by proxy, and the substitution of wealth and power for bodily and discursive integration. In his final and famous words, Gibbon uses the ancient formula of author as male mother, conceiving and delivering his work to his readers using the rhetoric of physical reproduction, but without any female agency. The trope of the author as male mother giving birth to his text is much older than Gibbon, but its relationship to the disembodied rhetoric of empire is especially clear here because of Gibbon's subject matter, and his placement of the trope at the emphatic position at the end of his work. (It is interesting to note the inversion of end and beginning that attends imperial rhetoric, in that Gibbon's text ends with an encapsulated narrative of its genesis.)

In Molly's text, history, geography, anatomy, the daily, monthly, and intermittent embodied narratives of elimination, bleeding, and desire and fulfillment, pulse together with thought, emotion, and the written word. Her final, triumphant sexual fantasy and satisfaction is fueled by her memories of her first lover, and her first sexual experience on the rock of Gibraltar, an experience in the past which is in no wise separate from the stimulation of nerve endings in the present. As Freud makes clear in his essay "Screen Memories," remembrance is frequently more about the present than the past:

> A "screen memory" [is] one which owes its value as a memory not to its own content but to the relation between that content and some other, that has been repressed... Anyone who bears in mind their distinctive feature—namely that they

are extremely well-remembered but that their content is completely indifferent—
will easily recall a number of examples of the sort from his own memory.[8]

The conscious narration of unconscious affect by way of writing acknowledges the role of the body in discourse, instead of trying to split it off. The body
and its textuality come together in Molly's discourse, and they are accompa-
nied by a third participant: the Rock. It is crucial to note that the body and its
text come together with not just place, but geology. Although a goal of empire
is frequently to extract wealth from conquered geology, imperial ambition is
famously detached from and ignorant of not only the land it wishes to exploit,
but also its own land of origin. Empire is alienated from earth, sea, and air as
well as from body. The rhetoric of abstraction that imperial conquest requires
also demands a severing of relationship with the ground. Part of the reason for
this is that there is a paradox of insecurity built into the rhetorical and physical
practice of colonization. It is dangerous to leave your doors unlocked in a neighborhood that you have bombed and pillaged. Once empire has begun its work
somewhere, it is left with no steady ground to rest on.

A body that remembers pleasure in language is able to transmute the
destructive effects of imperial work. This is what Joyce moves toward achieving
in "Penelope." "Gibraltar," one recalls, is a colloquial rendition of the Arabic
phrase Gebel al Tarik, or "Tarik's Mountain." "Gib," as Molly renders it, is also
her mountain, and in this regard it is useful to remember the *mons veneris*, or
mount of Venus, that anatomically refers to the turf of pleasure in a female
body, and even more specifically, to recall the promontory that makes orgasm
possible for women, the "little hill," or clitoris (Greek *kleitoris*). Stimulation
around Gibraltar brings Molly and the novel to a climax. What we have in
this discourse is the beginning of a new theory of power. Here the traumas
of history, body, and earth are integrated with pleasure by means of, incred-
ible as it may seem, *literature*, inasmuch as literature is, as Barbara Johnson has
written, "the work of making readable those impossible and necessary things
that cannot yet be spoken."[9]

By recounting this history over the stones of Gibraltar, Joyce begins a
process of rewriting empire that remains for other authors to complete. Molly's
discourse channels suggestions for the displacement of totalitarian structures
of dominance and control. Most evidently, the text insists on the way that the
body needs and also exceeds language. Rhetoric cannot stop a flow of blood.
But a female body can bleed and not die. Virginity, marriage, adultery, and faith-
fulness coincide in this one body, as do pleasure and pain. The cruelties and
ruptures of history are subject to some process of rearticulation and recreation
by way of playfully embodied language. And yet the female body carries all "the
force of this operation" in a way that other bodies do not.[10] Joyce has not found
a way to retell the story that does not involve making the body of woman work

for him. But the end of *Ulysses* does insist that the rock at the end of empire is both solid and shivered with pleasure.

Notes

1 James Joyce, *Ulysses*, ed. Hans Walter Gabler (New York: Random House, 1986), 643, ll. 1586–89.

2 For example, in his memoirs Gibbon insists that Henry Fielding's novel *Tom Jones* will outlast the Escorial (cited in *Bartlett's Familiar Quotations*, 340 a); in *Decline and Fall* he speaks of "those fortifications [on Gibraltar] which, in the hands of our countrymen, have resisted the art and power of the house of Bourbon" (3.195).

3 See Slavoj Žižek on this in *The Fragile Absolute, or, Why is the Christian Legacy Worth Fighting For?* (London: Verso, 2000).

4 Elizabeth Butler Cullingford, "Phoenician Genealogies and Oriental Geographies: Joyce, Language and Race," *Semicolonial Joyce*, ed. Derek Attridge and Marjorie Howes (Cambridge: Cambridge University Press, 2000), 229.

5 Ibid., 231.

6 Sigmund Freud, "The Uncanny" [1919], *The Standard Edition of the Complete Works of Sigmund Freud*, vol. 17, ed. and trans. James Strachey (London: The Hogarth Press, 1953), 245.

7 Hélène Cixous's dissertation on Joyce is a root of her theory of *écriture feminine* (*The Exile of James Joyce*, trans. Sally A. J. Purcell [London: John Calder Publishers, 1976]).

8 Sigmund Freud, "Screen Memories" [1899], *The Standard Edition of the Complete Works of Sigmund Freud*, vol. 3, ed. and trans. James Strachey (London: The Hogarth Press, 1953), 320.

9 Barbara Johnson, book-jacket blurb to *The Feminist Difference: Literature, Psychoanalysis, Race, and Gender*.

10 Jacques Derrida, cited in Mary Gossy, "Hymen and Text in *La Celestina*," *The Untold Story: Women and Theory in Golden Age Texts* (Ann Arbor, MI: The University of Michigan Press, 1989), 47.

CHAPTER THREE

The Stain of Spain in Some of Stein

When Gertrude Stein writes, in "Lifting Belly," "What is Spain," she enunciates a "declarative question" and creates a new grammatical trope that poses a question and states a fact at the same time.[1] The fact that is performed is the simultaneity of two terms in one time and space, without a loss of differentiation. It is not that the question says that it needs no answer, it is that it does not seek one. There is no answer sought, so there is no deferral into a future space where a lack might be filled. The declarative question constructs the familiar equivalence of terms on either side of the verb "to be:" "what" equals "Spain." The equation is also reversible; "Spain" is "what." In the declarative question, the mind remains suspended in an undefined certainty. This condition might be related to that of a mystical ecstasy of Divine Union, or marriage (as it is described, for example, by Stein's girlhood hero St. Teresa of Avila). Subject and object, question and answer do not collapse into one in this state. What does happen is that the "now" of the presence of difference becomes all-absorbing, and there is no departure from the moment of union, no lapse of attention in favor of a better, or more complete, moment.

If the declarative question is an announcement, the interrogative declaration might be read as an invitation. Again the commingling of the question and the statement of fact makes no demand, and does not seek (utopian) discursive plenitude. What does happen is that the statement opens itself to the embrace of a not knowing that is not traumatized or conflicted because of a desire for a final solution.

In reference to the erotic rhetoric of "Lifting Belly," the declarative question might be conceived of in a penetrative sense, the interrogative declaration in a receptive sense; but the kaleidoscopic confluence of the terms makes any attempt at dividing them into binarisms beside the point. It is, after all, the period, or full-stop, that makes this syntactic richness possible. The period is the punctuation mark that calmly moves beyond suspense and insists on the present moment, in which what has been written is being read. As a pun, the period makes cycles that reoccur but do not repeat, both as periodicity and difference, textualized in the flesh and blood of females. But to say that Stein's formulation performs the present moment (simultaneously, in various senses of incomplete fullness) is not to say that the writing is ahistorical or disembodied. In fact the declarative question and interrogative declaration make possible a holographic documentation of history and bodies because of their cubist capacity to perform multiple dimensions of meaning simultaneously. What is Spain, geographically, is the place and time where the writing of "Lifting Belly" is grounded. Stein began writing "Lifting Belly" in Mallorca in 1915, and completed it sometime in 1917. Mallorca is the largest of the Balearic Islands, and is politically part of Spain. Its history is both Spanish and non-Spanish; like Gibraltar it is neither here nor there, and both here and there.

Stein writes in this place in the middle of the Mediterranean ("middle-of-the-earth") Sea in the middle of the First World War, and the war is just as integral a part of the text as love-making. One critic has written that "'Lifting Belly' is [...] much more than an anthem of lesbian love. It is a story of lovers existing in a place and time of war."[2] But specificity is important here; "Lifting Belly" is a text about a specific kind of sexual relationship, in a specific time and place, in contexts of national war and domestic peace. As the war can be said to slip into the rooms of love, so can it be said that love finds its way onto the battlefield. In fact, this happens both in the text and in the bodily movements of Stein and Toklas; "Lifting Belly" goes to the war not to kill but to heal.[3] Stein and Toklas's love is prismatic; it is in bed, at the dining room table, and in the trenches all at once. The achievement here is stupendous; "Lifting Belly" incarnates the fact (in the sense of "deed") that erotic love between women saves lives in wartime. Their lovemaking is what fuels their rescuing vehicle.[4]

After their stay in Mallorca, Stein and Toklas leave for the south of France:

Is there a way of being careful
Of what.
Of the South.
By going to it.
We will go.
For them.
For them again.
And is there any likelihood of butter.
We do not need butter.
Lifting belly enormously and with song. (54)

"Going to it" is the way, not to get around it, but to love through it. And the structure of relationship that makes it possible to go to it is: "We will go. / For them. / For them again." "We," the erotic relationship, will go to it heroically. We will go "For them. / For them again" sacrificially, but consciously and tasting the fat, the rich, delicious song churned out by "Lifting belly enormously."

"What is Spain" also states the physical mystery that, as in the midst of milk there is butter, "In the midst of writing there is merriment." There is a phonetic double-entendre in "What is Spain." Read aloud, the sentence could be heard as "What is pain." The safe haven in Palma de Mallorca also inscribes *pain*, the embodied fact of war. But pain gives way to merriment because it is impossible not to continue past the English word to the French "pain," bread, which was, buttered and unbuttered, in the mouths, on the lips and the laps of Gertrude and Alice all the time. It is the consecration of their love-feast. Spain, pain, *pain*: the text finds a way to bring France and Spain into conversation, by acknowledging both distress and the necessity of sitting down together for a good meal.

This "Spain" (this pain/*pain*) appears in "Lifting Belly" ten times in the form of Spanish words, the words "Spain" or "Spanish," or Spanish place names. Spain and people and things Spanish figure prominently in many of Stein's works. But references to Spain in "Lifting Belly" form a constellation of allusion that enacts, again, an unmerged simultaneity of erotic, political, and aesthetic meaning. "The Cataluna has come home" refers to a ship that could not return to the harbor because of the war (14). But of course the sentence also contains the expression "The Cat has come home," a banal and reassuring domestic announcement. Beloved felines wander off, sometimes never to reappear; "The Cat has come home" allays anxiety and restores order. The Spanish imperial enterprise makes an appearance, too:

> Lifting belly is so long.
> It is an expression of opinion.
> Conquistador. James I
> It is exceptional.
> Lifting belly is current rolling. Lifting belly is so strong.
> Lifting belly is so strong. (15)

"James I," in the sense of "James the First," alludes historically to the late-thirteenth and early-fourteenth-century (1243–1311) king of Mallorca. A reader familiar with English literature and history will also think of the son of Mary, Queen of Scots, and Lord Darnley (1566–1625), who became King of England and whose name is enshrined in the literary record because he authorized a translation of the Bible, known everywhere as the King James version. The allusion would seem to have its strongest historical connection to James the Conqueror (Jaime el Conquistador), King of Aragon and (re-)conqueror of the Balearic Islands, who wrested them from the Moors in the early thirteenth century, and was the ruler who made those islands specifically Spanish. But it is in terms of the graphical quality of the sentence that a prismatic effect is most clearly seen. "James I" can also be read as "James I" [as a first-person pronoun, thus pronounced "James Eye"]. The Caesars of other verses have become a specific, Mallorcan, erotic conqueror and seer/see-er. It is tempting even to read the capitalized letter "i" with its Spanish pronunciation, which would make it "ee." Then the phrase would be "James ee," bizarrely foreshadowing Molly Bloom's statement in the Penelope chapter of *Ulysses*, in which she expresses her exasperation at her menstrual flow: "O Jamesy let me up out of this pooh."[5] In any case, this conqueror operates both in a specific place and time (Mallorca in the thirteenth century and at the beginning of the twentieth), and across place, time, connotation, language, and definition. "James Eye" says what it sees, which is more than any one reader can read. James I demands reading in relationship, and proposes a new kind of conquest, in which the capacity to read many languages simultaneously opens new territory without creating domination. "We go to Barcelona to-morrow" but not today (16). "We go" (in the present) to Barcelona (not here) tomorrow (not today). The places and times invoked have differing valences of importance, but they all work to support a discourse of a present that permeates past and future. But Stein phrases it better in "Four Saints in Three Acts": "There is a difference between Barcelona and Avila. What difference. There is a difference between Barcelona and Avila. / There is a difference between Barcelona."[6] "Lifting Belly" twice mentions Avila, the city of Saint Teresa: "Did you say third. No I said Avila" (18); and, "Listen to me. Using old automobile tires as sandals is singularly interesting. It is done in Avila" (19). "No I said Avila" returns to the multiple meanings of "James I." The sentence can be read as "No, I said Avila," "No I (meaning no one, or I (the Roman numeral)) said Avila," i.e., "nobody said Avila." (The pun is reminiscent of the Cyclops's cry, "No man is killing me!" The word "Avila" can further be sounded as "a villa" (a city, a house).

Avila stands atop a hill in Old Castile. It is surrounded and protected by a high red wall and 88 original eleventh-century towers. It is an impregnable fortress town whose massive beautiful walls and towers are echoed by the wall of rock of the Sierra de Gredos behind it. It is a dry place. The land's surface is straw-colored, the surface rarely broken, unless for a solitary cypress or poplar. The sky, winter and summer, is a relentless, clear, desert blue. The city stretches across the breast of one of the bare, long, rolling hills that heave across the landscape until they break into the snow-capped peaks of the Gredos range. It is easy to understand Alice's reaction to the city:

> We went straight to Avila, and I immediately lost my heart to Avila, I must stay in Avila forever I insisted. Gertrude Stein was very upset, Avila was alright but, she insisted, she needed Paris. I felt that I needed nothing but Avila. We were both very violent about it. We did however stay there for ten days and as Saint Theresa was a heroine of Gertrude Stein's youth we thoroughly enjoyed it. In the opera Four Saints written a few years ago she describes the landscape that so profoundly moved me.[7]

"No I said Avila" has all of the lovers' passion and conflict in it. In *Lectures in*

America, Stein says that she "made the saints the landscape" in "Four Saints in Three Acts."[8] St. Therese, as Stein spells the name in this text, is the saint who makes the most appearances in "Four Saints." Her secular name was Teresa de Cepeda y Alumada and her religious name Teresa de Jesus, but she is known to the faithful and to history as Teresa of Avila—for decades she traveled all over Spain; she invoked a sense of homelessness in her saying "life is like a night spent in a bad hotel," but her body and the city are inseparable. Stein insists again and again on the specificity of place, time, and body in the making of this new mode of discourse. Avila is a fortified city that St. Teresa protected carefully through the ages by taking it out on the road in her mission to establish enclosed convents where women in community could open themselves in solitary ecstasy to the everywhere and nowhere, and also to the right here-and-now of divine union. The fortified city and wide open abandonment to love happen together. St. Teresa and Avila, like "Lifting Belly," make new ways of remaking love and war: "If it were possible to kill five thousand chinamen by pressing a button would it be done. / Saint Therese not interested."[9] Love is not a matter for the subjunctive. Stein calls out the declarative present tense: "It is done in Avila" (19). What specifically is done in Avila is the impossible:

> Magpies are in the landscape that is they are in the sky of a landscape, they are black and white and they are in the landscape in Bilignin and in Spain, especially in Avila. When they are in the sky they do something I have never seen any other bird do they hold themselves up and down and look flat against the sky.
> A very famous French inventor of things that have to do with stabilisation in aviation told me that what I told him magpies did could not be done by any bird but anyway whether the magpies at Avila do do it or do not at least they look as if they do do it. They look exactly like the birds in the Annunciation pictures the bird which is the Holy Ghost and rests flat against the sky very high.[10]

The virgin birth alluded to by the mention of the Annunciation is the moment in which the physically impossible incarnates. The birds in Avila do the physically impossible. Stein has seen the impossible done, and she has written it down. Miracles and sanctity are found in all kinds of places; writing the love between women impregnates war with peace.

Notes

1 Gertrude Stein, "Lifting Belly," *The Yale Gertrude Stein*, selections by Richard Kostelanetz (New Haven, CT: Yale University Press, 1980), 50. All internal citations refer to this edition.

2 David M. Owens, "Gertrude Stein's 'Lifting Belly' and The Great War," *Modern Fiction Studies* 44.3 (1998): 608.

3 Ibid., 617.

4 In fact, Stein and Toklas used their car, which they named "Auntie," to do relief work during the war.

5 Joyce, *Ulysses*, 633.

6 Gertrude Stein, "Four Saints in Three Acts" [1929], *Selected Writings of Gertrude Stein*, ed. Carl Van Vechten (New York: Vintage Books, 1990), 607.

7 Gertrude Stein, *The Autobiography of Alice B. Toklas*, *Selected Writings of Gertrude Stein*, ed. Carl Van Vechten (New York: Vintage Books, 1990), 108–09.

8 Gertrude Stein quoted from Carl Van Vechten's introductory note to "Four Saints in Three Acts," 578.

9 Stein, "Four Saints," 586.

10 Gertrude Stein, *Lectures in America*; cited by Carl Van Vechten in his introductory note to "Four Saints in Three Acts," 578–79.

CHAPTER FOUR

Lesbian Hymen-mending by *Celestina* and Wittig

"Can it be that I still long for my virginity?"
—Sappho, Book IX, *Wedding Songs*, no. 159

Oh noche que juntaste
amado con amada
amada en el amado transformada

[Oh you night that joined
Butch with femme
Femme in the butch transfemmed][1]
—S. Juan de la Cruz, "Noche oscura," stanza 5

The author's note to the English translation of Monique Wittig's *The Lesbian Body* says that

> The body of the text subsumes all the words of the female body. *Le Corps Lesbien* attempts to achieve the affirmation of its reality. The lists of names contribute to this activity. To recite one's own body, to recite the body of the other, is to recite the words of which the book is made up.[2]

Within the text, lists of anatomical names for parts of the lesbian body interweave with the narratives that describe the mutual dismembering and remembering of the lovers J/e and tu. These lists do not break up the narrative rhythm, but rather support it like a backbeat. The lists' recitation of names of body parts echoes the lists of proper names of amazons in Wittig's *Les Guérillères*: the simple, repetitive naming of names, without metaphoric or stylistic embellishment—other than their linear ordering—has the effect of ritually concretizing the reality signified, or, as the quotation says, of "affirming the reality" of the amazons or of the lesbian body.

Les Guérillères, unlike *Le Corps Lesbien*, is not preceded in the original or in the English translation by any statement that claims comprehensiveness: it does not seek to name all amazons. I was struck, then, by the mention in the Author's Note that "the body of the text" of *Le Corps Lesbien* "subsumes all the words of the female body." It is true that the text is remarkably thorough in its naming or mentioning of parts of the female body, and this mentioning has the effect of reclaiming the body from the fetishizing practices of patriarchal sexual economies: the lesbian body is not anatomized into its pornographic elements, it is (and here I chose a page at random, as I was writing, to exclude all but the most arcane unconscious fetishizations on my own part): "ligature, belly, sex, armpits, skin, ears, swellings, head, foot, pelvis, bust" (78–79). And it is also "occiput, trapezii, cerebrospinal fluid, cerebellum" (17). (That series I chose more intentionally, to show the use of Latinate anatomical terminology.) Thus, the body parts traditionally fetishized by patriarchy appear, but as part of a whole, and not isolated as especially significant. It might be argued that a certain fetishization is taking place in the fact that the vulva is named thrice, and the vagina twice, but the repetition is unobtrusive; rather than to call attention to the parts, the extra invocation is necessary to call these parts, the conduits of appropriation, back from their excessive exile.

The vulva, the vagina, breasts, feet, mouth, anus, and other parts of the female body most singled out for fetishization are all mentioned in the text or in the lists. For this reason it was surprising to discover that another part of the body that is subject to symbolic appropriation, and precisely right at the moment of initial accession to heterosexual genital sexuality, is not named in the book. I had hoped to see the hymen reclaimed in the text by this naming, and it is not. The missing hymen troubled me, not least because I was confronting its absence from the text as a gap I wanted to fill. This would not be a problem if I had not written elsewhere that as readers we have been taught or acculturated to treat gaps in narrative as fetishized feminine objects—that is, as holes in the texts, defects that must be filled in with "acts of ideation," [3] or at the least, properly probed. A way to read gaps that does not participate in this economy could be to let them mean in their (apparent) emptiness, to elicit meaning from the detail surrounding the gap rather than to inscribe or to decide it. So there are at least two problems. The first is that by looking for "hymen" where it is not written, I too may be participating in its exploitation. The second is that since I have one in my own female body, and think that it is a body part that has been overdetermined by and stolen from me by patriarchal meaning systems, I want it to be reclaimed in and with the body of Wittig's text. I want it to be named as are vulva and occiput, and it is not. Like vulva, vagina, and other stolen parts and words, it is too meaningful in the patriarchal economy to be left unnamed, or unmeaning, in *Le Corps Lesbien*. This latter observation leads me to believe that the hymen is important not only in my own unconscious, but also in that of the text.

In *Lesbian Peoples: Material for a Dictionary*, Wittig and Sande Zeig explicitly address the issue of gaps, in the entry "Dictionary":

> The arrangement of the dictionary allows us to eliminate those elements which
> have distorted our history during the dark ages, from the Iron Age to the Glorious
> Age. The arrangement could be called lacunary. [It also permits utilization of the
> lacunae as litotes in a sentence where one says the least to say the most.][4]

To go from dictionary to dictionary, *American Heritage* says that litotes is a "figure
of speech consisting in an understatement in which an affirmative is expressed
by negating its opposite, as in *This is no small problem*."[5] Indeed it is not. If lacunae,
by saying nothing, say the most, then the text runs the risk of having what it does
express shouted down by what it represses, which says more. It is the function
of the untold, as narratological entity, that is, that part of a text whose absence
calls attention to it, to undermine the orthodoxy, or the expressed consistency,
of the narrative of which it is a part. But the expressed narrative also depends
upon the untold for its form and process.

Thus, *The Lesbian Body* cannot write hymen without undermining its project
as a "text written by women exclusively for women, careless of male approval,"
for "Women who live among themselves and for themselves at all the generally
accepted levels: fictional, symbolic, actual" (9). Hymen must be elided because it
is the place where the reclamation of traditional anatomical terms that proceeds
so beautifully and redemptively throughout *Le Corps Lesbien* does not work. Vulva
means vulva, or for the etymologically inclined, vulva, cover, wrapper. Vagina
means vagina, or sheath or scabbard. Clitoris means clitoris, or little hill. The
etymological origins of these words do not compromise their contemporary
connotative field, or their invocation in a symbolic economy to which patriarchy
is irrelevant. But hymen, when it says hymen, says marriage and virginity. As
such it has been appropriated and fetishized by critical theory. For Derrida, for
example, it incarnates the between of a text, that part of a text that is undecidable. In *Dissemination*, "hymen" is the incarnation of *entre*, the between:

> ... if we replaced "hymen" by "marriage" or "crime," "identity" or "difference," etc.,
> the effect would be the same, the only loss being a certain economic condensation
> or accumulation, which has not gone unnoticed. It is the "between," whether it
> names fusion or separation, that thus carries all the force of the operation.[6]

But as I have written before,

> Another loss would be the loss of the metaphor to phallic transgression;
> metaphorically, a hymen in a vagina "carries all the force of the operation" [of
> phallic analysis] in a way that the alternatives that Derrida suggests do not.[7]

There is a flesh and blood, nervy body involved here. "The importance of
the tissue-text called hymen to marriage and virginity is made up, a fiction."[8]
The coincidence of meaning, of Hymen as pagan god of Marriage and of the
organ, hymen, as the guarantor of virginity, makes for a good story. (It is the
story of the domination of women, but that will come later.) "If either one

[marriage or non-consummation] did take place, there would be no hymen," insists Derrida[9]—to which I now want to reply, partly because of the expression "white wedding," "Mariage Blanc"—"but there is Blanche, there is!" As anatomy books remind us, even after having penetrative heterosexual vaginal sex for the first time, and bleeding all over the bed (or not, as is very common); even after those infamous encounters with rowdy saddle pommels or the top frames of boys' bicycles, even after giving birth by vaginal delivery, for goodness' sake, "little folds of hymen tissue remain."[10] Officially these are called tags, or even more officially, caruncles. After all these operations, interpretive and otherwise, "there is still a body" and marriage and virginity are "irrelevant to the hymen *qua* hymen."[11] What this means is "the possibility of woman as subject";[12] in the context of the works under discussion here, it also means "the possibility of lesbian"—as subject, or at all.

There seems to be an insistence, in reading and other ways of living, that the hymen in the text or in the body be written over, and broken. Why? In most women, it is already open—if it were not, menstrual blood could not pass through. So the hymen fiction again rewrites anatomy for metaphor. But there is a way of reading hymens that rewrites this fiction that undoes women's bodies and subjectivities. (And if it is tough on women, you can be sure that it will be twice as hard on lesbians.)

Castration, as it is understood in psychoanalytic film theory, puts the phallus first. In fact, as Teresa de Lauretis writes in *Alice Doesn't*, castration and its hair- (and other body-part) raising effects (by way of allusion to Freud's short essay "Medusa's Head") may be, fundamentally, what makes cinema possible.[13] Castration is what works in traditional film narrative. At the foundation of all the layers the gazing eye negotiates when looking at the screen, there is the phallus. Renegotiating castration is the fun of cinema, for many, many people. The Oedipus complex is resolved again, to everyone's temporary relief. But the satisfaction is brief, and thus allows for the proliferation of formulaic films. I would like to suggest another way to watch movies. I am not sure that every-body is up to it, but it is worth explaining, because it is related to how new forms of narrative, filmed or written, may be produced.

It has been commonly said that lesbians are stuck at the pre-Oedipal phase, in a dyadic, erotic attachment to the mother, that lesbians have somehow not negotiated castration or completed the work of Oedipal transitions. I think that a specifically lesbian gaze has worked through the Oedipal, and that it can and does see castration for what it is, a powerful fiction. I also think that what is different about the lesbian gaze is that it sees *through* castration, literally. Castration is there—translucent, perhaps transparent, maybe a membrane, even—and seen through it is a vulva that was not phallic in the first place— even if it is "where the phallus has been."[14] A lesbian gaze can *see* the vulva *qua* vulva that castration (seen alone) makes invisible. Castration puts the phallus first. Seeing through castration makes another economy of representation possible.

Heather Findlay's, "Is there a Lesbian in this Text? Derrida, Wittig, and the Politics of the Three Women" addresses the question in terms of *The Lesbian Body*. Among other myths resurrected by Wittig in her text is that of Isis and Osiris. In Wittig's text, the two lovers making and unmaking each other are like these protagonists of Egyptian myth, except that when Isis goes to reconstruct Osiris in *The Lesbian Body*,

> There is no missing thirteenth piece, instead there are thirteen pieces which are constantly lost and found. Whereas castration is clearly negated, it is also affirmed *in a new sense...*[15]

This new sense could have to do precisely with the capacity to see castration and to see past or through it: what is lost and found and lost and found again is never really lost—it is more like a game of peek-a-boo, which may be more subversive and revolutionary as a representational strategy than heretofore imagined. The fun is in knowing that what seemed lost is on its way back, that what goes around comes around. Humpty-Dumpty *can* be put back together again, and Humpty can fall down and break again. Singing the nursery rhyme over and over (you never sing a nursery rhyme once) reconstitutes Humpty fully. I see how these nursery strategies may be used to enforce traditional views of castration, and I also see how they can serve to rewrite it to make more space for what some forms of power want to smash.

Like Humpty-Dumpty, people fall off walls in the *Tragicomedia de Calisto y Melibea*, otherwise and most commonly known by the name of its protagonist, Celestina. In fact, the constant up and down movement in the text is one of its great themes. The relation between this text and *The Lesbian Body* is not as distant as it seems. Celestina's attentions to her female coworkers is something other than heterosexual; she delights in palpating their naked youthfulness. Also, for a woman to mend hymens is something other than heterosexual— physically to do it, one woman has to put her hand inside another woman. In *Celestina's Brood: Continuities of the Baroque in Spanish and Latin American Literature*, Roberto González-Echevarría writes that the *Celestina* as a whole is still in need of all kinds of readings; that its meanings for today's readers have yet to be explicated. González-Echevarría too sees something new and strange going on in the *Celestina*'s narrative strategies. As I mentioned before, I would add *Don Quijote*, Cervantes's *Novelas ejemplares*, and *Le Corps Lesbien* to the list (among others), all as precursors of as yet unwritten narratives that do not depend upon the destruction of women as their motive force. I would even call them radical new forms of representation—from 1499, 1605, and 1615, and the even more strangely distant year of 1973 (the year *Le Corps Lesbien* was first published in France). Yet González finds Celestina's work to be purely destructive. He understands that "The mended hymen is, then, a text woven by Celestina as a counterfiction."[16] I am not sure that "counterfiction" is the best word for the made and unmade, made and unmade hymen-text, but for the moment let it suffice. But the critic cannot see the life-giving properties of this activity: "The mended hymen is a text, even an emblem of the text of Celestina, but as such it is made up by puncturing, rending, bleeding, and a general disfigurement."[17] "Puncturing, rending, bleeding, and general disfiguring" is what the lovers in *The Lesbian Body* do to each other, precisely in the process of making, unmaking, and remaking narrative:

> You are exsanguinated. All your blood torn forcibly from your limbs issues violently from your groins carotid arms temples legs ankles, the arteries are crudely severed, it involves the carotids brachials radials temporals, it involves the iliacs femorals tibials peroneals, the veins are simultaneously laid open. (20–21)

It may be important to remember here that it is biologically normal for women to bleed, sometimes quite profusely, for a large part of their lives, and to do so without dying. It may not be pretty to a gaze structured by castration anxiety, but what happens in *The Lesbian Body* and *Celestina* is intrinsic to the production of a new kind of narrative. González does mention this when he writes of Celestina's brew as a kind of Derridean *pharmakon*, and adds that "The mythic substratum of *Celestina* is composed of these figures [mythical Eastern figures and stories] who seem to inhabit the origin of writing and of literature."[18] Exactly what is it that she does? Pármeno, once her ward, tells us:

> Esto de los virgos, unos hacía de vejiga y otros curaba de punto. Tenía en un tabladillo, en una cajuela pintada, unas agujas delgadas de pellejeros e hilos de seda encerados, y colgadas allí raíces de hojaplasma y fuste sanguino, cebolla albarrana y cepacaballo; hacía con esto maravillas: que cuando vino por aquí el embajador frances, tres veces vendió por virgen una criada que tenía.[19]

> In the matter of maidenheads—some she made of bladder, some she sewed. In a little painted chest on a stand she had some thin needles such as leatherworkers use, and waxed silk threads, and there were roots of hojaplasma and fuste sanguino, squill, and cardoon. She worked wonders with these, and when the French ambassador was here she sold him as a virgin three times over the same one of her servants. (C, 36)

But she does not mend hymens only for profit:

> Y remediaba por caridad muchas huérfanas y erradas que se encomendaban a ella; (C, 62)

> [And out of charity she helped many orphans and errant girls who came to her (C, 36).]

Sometimes she does it to save lives. Her hymen-text-making, as an operation done under the cover of her profession as town seamstress and go-between and curandera, keeps the text moving. If she had been alive to mend the heroine Melibea's hymen after the latter's ill-fated sexual encounter with her lover Calisto, Melibea would never have jumped from a tower to her death. If we had the new narratives prefigured by *Celestina*, maybe hymen-mending would no longer be necessary. If we start with the convenient date of *Celestina*'s text (assuredly there was hymen-mending before, but just for the sake of argument), 1499, we have just about completed 500 years of hymen-mending, with no end in sight. The problem is, it happens to embodied women, not only literary characters. In the summer of 1999 the 20-hour, 400-year-old Chinese opera "The Peony Pavilion" was featured at Lincoln Center. One of its burlesque characters is a nun named Sister Stone, "known for her unbreakable hymen."[20] But *Deutsche Presse-Agentur* also reports in 1994 that "growing numbers of sexually active Chinese women are seeking to surgically regain their virginity" and that "Many hospitals have recently started performing operations to restore women's hymens. The *China Women's News* said two Beijing hospitals have attracted more than 100 customers in their first four months of doing the operation." And all this is happening even though the medical personnel involved "say than an unbroken hymen is not necessarily a sign of virginity since it can be broken through sports or other physical activity."[21] The official line in China still sees this emphasis on hymen = virgin as evidence of a sexual double standard, but women with the cash and the option ("customers", as the article states), still seek the appearance of virginity. The implication in this article is that the hymen-mending verges on cosmetic surgery, at least for these Chinese women. Not so for women in other parts of the world. The *Lancet* reported in 1996 that Egypt was "becoming an Arab centre for performing illegal operations of hymen repair."[22] In Egypt this involves suturing a gelatin capsule containing a blood-like substance into the vagina, "so that when it bursts during intercourse on the wedding night, the groom will be convinced that his bride is a virgin." The textuality of the event is noted in the next sentence, which states that "According to custom, a blood-stained white silk handkerchief is then displayed to close female family members waiting outside the bedroom." All this is necessary because "a woman who is not found to be a virgin on her wedding night will bring great shame on her family. In rural areas, the woman is killed, thereby 'cleansing the shame.' This task is undertaken by the woman's brothers, uncles, or even her father." Nevertheless,

> the operation has [also] been condemned by Al Azhar, Egypt's highest Muslim religious body. It has been described as 'cheating' since much Muslim tradition insists that brides be virgins. However, some policemen are claiming that in the past ten years use of the operation has reduced by 80% the number of murders committed to cleanse the honour of wronged families.[23]

In other words, hymen-mending is not an ideal solution, but you get to live.

There is a report in the February 7, 1998 *British Medical Journal* about the ethics of hymen reconstruction in the Netherlands. The operation there is an outpatient procedure involving an interpreter and social worker as well as the medical personnel. "The hymenal remnants are adapted by a circular running suture or by left to right approximation. Where the hymenal remnants are insufficient, a narrow strip of posterior vaginal wall is dissected for reconstruction."[24] There is a follow up at three weeks, and the patient is offered the opportunity to remove or destroy any notes on this procedure from her medical record. The Dutch doctors distinguish between their methods of hymen-mending and clitoridectomy by saying that "hymen reconstruction is not mutilating; the risk of physical, psychological, and sexual complications is far less than in clitoridectomy."[25] They see it as a form of "ritualistic surgery" which in their definition is "fulfillment of a person's need rather than a response to their medical condition" and compare "the ethics of hymen reconstruction [...] to the ethics of cosmetic surgery, an accepted part of plastic and reconstructive surgery worldwide." In 2005 some of my graduate students brought me advertisements from a Queens, New York Spanish-language newspaper which featured surgical hymen-mending; and as of 2007 hymenoplasty is one of the most sought-after "cosmetic" surgical procedures in the world. On the psychic level, there is the so-called Born Again Virgin movement, in which girls and young women who have had sex, and lost their virginity, decide to return to traditional evangelical Christian norms of pre- and extra-marital celibacy. In this context, "being saved" also rhetorically, if not physically, restores the hymen of the woman in question.[26]

With these contemporary narratives, the question of economic class enters the picture. The surgical operations are expensive. One woman feigned insanity for four months while she was saving up for the operation.[27] There is no mention of gynecologists in Egypt or the Netherlands or China doing the operation for free for "orphaned girls" or other "errant women" the way Celestina does. I go on at some length about these contemporary cases because they describe so clearly the old intersection between text and sex. But what is missing from the contemporary clinical narratives is the interweaving and textmaking evident in the *Celestina*. Perhaps what is most grievously absent is the knowledge that virginity is a fiction, and that these operations are not the only way to go, at least for some women. It is possible to do things in fiction that cannot or need not be carried out in real life, but fiction can make it possible to reimagine what is possible in real life, under given material conditions. "It is our fiction that validates us," says the Author's Note to *The Lesbian Body* (10). It expresses "The desire to bring the real body violently to life in the words of the book (everything that is written exists)" (10). For Wittig, this is a person/body/lesbian who is "*intact*" as well as made and unmade, but without reference to a hymen: "When you stop m/y darling, you will have spongy matter on your hands and on your arms viscosities, pitch putrescence blood lymph bile *you my most intact*" (155, my emphasis).

In an early essay on Beauvoir, Wittig, and Foucault, Judith Butler mentions that "we might do well to urge speculation on the dynamic relation between fantasy and the realization of new social realities."[28] I would say that this is what literature (and maybe even literary criticism), but specifically the work of reading and writing literature can do: change things for lesbians. It is almost thirty years since Wittig wrote in that same Author's Note that:

> *Le Corps Lesbien* has lesbianism as its theme, that is, a theme which cannot even be described as taboo, for it has no real existence in the history of literature. Male homosexual literature has a past, it has a present. The lesbians, for their part, are silent—just as all women are as women at all levels. When one has read the poems of Sappho, Radclyffe Hall's *Well of Loneliness*, the poems of Sylvia Plath and Anais Nin, *La Batarde* by Violette Leduc, one has read everything. Only the women's movement has proved capable of producing lesbian texts in a context of total rupture with masculine culture, texts written by women exclusively for women, careless of male approval. *Le Corps Lesbien* falls into this category. (9)

Now, at the beginning of the twenty-first century, lesbian literature has a history, and a criticism. Much has been learned, and achieved, much pleasure given and taken. But Butler also reminds the reader of "the Marxist qualification [that] reinforces the notion that how we are constituted is not always our own affair."[29] One might extract from this observation a connection with Wittig's conclusion to *The Straight Mind*: "Lesbians are not women."[30] Wittig might know that lesbians are not women, and you and I might know that lesbians are not women, but the Man in the street does not know that lesbians are not women. In the context of the street (Celestina's favorite haunt), the lesbian is either too much or too little. Either way, this leads to the infamous problem of lesbian invisibility. Thus, as Leigh Gilmore has it in her essay on Jeannette Winterson's *Written on the Body* and *The Lesbian Body* (and she alludes here to Terry Castle), "the lesbian is typically represented as a ghostly presence, a specter whose haunting is evidence of both her derealization and her persistent presence."[31] In a note to this paragraph, Gilmore mentions that in some contexts, "Writing [...] merely drapes the real [...]"[32] This comment leads me to two questions: are lesbians veiled, as by a gaze that posits castration as foundational? Or are lesbians the veil itself? The veil and the hymen, of course, are closely linked in marriage symbolism. At another point, Butler's essay says that "the denial of the body is the embodiment of denial."[33] This leads me to think that the hymen, in the contexts I have been discussing, is a ghost; that women can and do bleed without dying; that is, women, in an economy that believes in ghosts, are ghostly; and that the almost invisible lesbian is the most ghostly creature of all. There is a connotative field that holds the meanings "ghost," "lesbian invis-ibility," and "hymen" together.

Where Wittig names and renames, and Celestina makes and unmakes, Jeanette Winterson will not name. Her protagonist in *Written on the Body* is unnamed and un-gendered, as is curiously (at least according to my argument) the protago-nist of Cristina Peri Rossi's *Solitario de amor* (1988). In reference to this, Gilmore asks, "in what ways does a name indicate presence? Must the absence of a name be linked to loss? [...] when and how can absence be read as something other than loss?"[34] Gilmore continues,

> These questions [in this case, how great is the space between the names woman and lesbian] all concern the interpretive space opened up between sexuality and gender, between identity and names. And it is a space that Winterson *will not suture* [my emphasis]. Since Winterson will not *suture* this space, what meanings are generated and circulate here?"[35]

I cannot read the word "suture" here without thinking of hymen-mending. At issue is the relation between this suture or non-suture and visibility or invis-ibility of a lesbian in the text. Have we made sufficient progress or change in practices of representation that, in this case, no suture is necessary—that a suture, in fact would be superfluous at best, painful and irrevocably annihi-lating at worst? Are we in fifteenth-century Spain, Cairo, in twenty-first-century Queens, New York, or a suburban U.S. rally of Born Again Virgins? Or is it Paris in the Springtime of 1968?

Gilmore has the impressive insight that in Wittig, at least, the suture is irrel-evant because the Lesbian Body exists in terms of a fractal geometry, instead of in terms of synecdoche. That is,

> Fractal geometry offers a way to describe irregular shapes (sometimes called "pathological" in Euclidean geometry) that are self-similar, i.e., are shaped identi-cally at their micro- and macro-levels. [...] The lesbian body at every order is identical in morphology to every other order of magnitude. Each part is identical to any other part in shape, and therefore the body can be recognized as lesbian from *any* fragment and can also regenerate the largest organization of the body from any fragment.[36]

Making and unmaking virgins the way Celestina does, making and unmaking body/love the way *The Lesbian Body* does, is playing with this fractal geometry to make new narrative shapes. Perhaps for this reason Gilmore says that "In its conclusion *Written on the Body* appears to be more prequel than sequel to *The Lesbian Body*."[37] Perhaps *The Lesbian Body* is a prequel to the *Celestina*: speaking in terms of the fractal, *The Lesbian Body* is a hymen, and Celestina takes up where Wittig leaves off, making and unmaking in a context that takes both narrative and social consequences into account.

What is still new in Wittig and, parenthetically, Winterson, is the knowledge that the hymen makes *heterosexuality* but does not *unmake* lesbian sexuality. It is unnamed in Wittig (unnamed like Winterson's narrator), and it is unnamed like hundreds of other parts. Yet in both cases it is *explicitly* unnamed. What happens to sexualities if the hierarchies of sexualized parts are disturbed or reconfigured, rewritten or abolished? What if there is no hymen to break or not to break, no marriage, no virginity? This constant negation is leading me back to the epigraph from St. John of the Cross that, with Sappho's, opens this essay:

O noche que juntaste
amado con amada
amada en el amado transformada.

The beloved amada (the feminine) is transformed in el Amado (the masculine), but in Spanish the (feminine) *a* remains at the end of *transformada* to specify the limits of the transformation. That little *a* is the hymen that goes beyond narrative convention. It is the body that exceeds the written.

It might be argued that where there is no hymen, that is, either consummation or virginity, there is no woman. So not only are lesbians not women, but some women are not women, either. This is forty years of progress. And yet, as we have seen, there is still plenty of hymen mending in 2009. The body still matters, theoretically and more than theoretically. A friend of mine, who died a few years ago, shortly before her death described herself as "deeply closeted" and thus, in her thinking, painfully affected by discourses and practices of misogyny and homophobia. She was not killed by homophobia, but still it made a difference to her life finally to meet a lesbian who had made and unmade her own in-ing and out-ing hundreds of times, and to find a space and place in which she could pronounce the words, "I'm gay." The nerves that hurt can be soothed by a text that is not afraid to make and unmake itself; this sneaky Celestinesque making and unmaking can literally be life-giving within oppressive systems, while, weaving along, it gradually undoes them, too.

Notes

1 "amada en el amado transformada" describes the change that divine union effects on the "amada," here translated as "femme." Christian mystical theology has traditionally considered the soul as feminized-Beloved in relation to a masculinized God-Lover. And yet traditional readings also sometimes ascribe activity to females,"women," and the feminine and passivity to males, "men," and the masculine. The passive and active roles of divine lovers have been closely connected to conceptions of femininity and masculinity in a way that mirrors the early Freud's thinking about infantile sexuality and its development toward normative heterosexuality. These terms can then be, and have been, required of and enacted on male, female, and otherwise sexed human bodies. Nevertheless, the *Song of Songs* (or "Song of Solomon") has Lover, Beloved, and seemingly choral voices that have confounded centuries of readers and translators who have sought to make binary readings

of the text. Many contemporary bibles separate sections into conjectured "roles" of Lover (masculine), Beloved (feminine), and "Friends," or a similar term for a chorus of maidens. What is most striking is in fact the role play involved in divine love, the willingness to step into a dance and to play within variable forms. Pushing this idea to a limit, I have used the terms "butch" and "femme,' further trying to get the strangeness of the last word of the citation, "transformada"—a transformation has taken place (as in the moment of hymen as both virginity and consummation), but that "a" remains at the end, continuing to mark the transformed being as something between changed and the same—that is, as something whose difference continues as ever the slide from binarism.

2 Monique Wittig, *The Lesbian Body*, trans. David Le Vay (Boston: Beacon Press, 1986 [1975]), 10. All internal citations refer to this edition.

3 See Wolfgang Iser, *The Act of Reading: A Theory of Aesthetic Response* (Baltimore, MD: Johns Hopkins University Press, 1978).

4 Monique Wittig and Sande Zeig, *Lesbian Peoples: Material for a Dictionary* (New York: Avon, 1979), 43.

5 "litotes," *The American Heritage Dictionary* (Boston: Houghton Mifflin, 4th ed., 2000).

6 Mary Gossy, *The Untold Story: Women and Theory in Golden Age Texts* (Ann Arbor, MI: University of Michigan Press, 1989), 47.

7 Ibid.

8 Ibid., 48.

9 Ibid.

10 *Our Bodies, Ourselves*, cited in Gossy, *The Untold Story*, 48.

11 Gossy, *The Untold Story*, 48.

12 Ibid.

13 Teresa de Lauretis, "Desire in Narrative," *Alice Doesn't: Feminism, Semiotics, Cinema* (London: Macmillian, 1984).

14 Barbara Johnson, "Aesthetic and Rapport in Toni Morrison's *Sula*," *The Feminist Difference: Literature, Psychoanalysis, Race, and Gender* (Cambridge, MA: Harvard University Press, 1998), PP ref?.

15 Heather Findlay, "Is there a Lesbian in this Text? Derrida, Wittig, and the Politics of the Three Women," *Coming to Terms: Feminism, Theory, Politics*, ed. Elizabeth Weed (New York: Routledge, 1989), 68; emphasis added.

16 Roberto González-Echevarría, *Celestina's Brood: Continuities of the Baroque in Spanish and Latin American Literature* (Durham, NC: Duke University Press, 1993), 26.

17 Ibid.

18 Ibid., 34.

19 Fernando de Rojas, *La Celestina; tragicomedia de Calisto y Melibea*, ed. Dorothy S. Severin (Madrid: Alianza Editorial, 1969), 62. All internal citations refer to this edition.

20 David Patrick Stearns, "Long, Long Opera, Fallible Characters Demand Attention," *USA Today*, July 13, 1999, sec. 4D

21 "More Chinese Women Seek to Regain Virginity," *Deutsche Presse-Agentur*, December 14, 1994.

22 Peter Kandela, "Egypt's Trade in Hymen Repair," *The Lancet* 47 (June 8, 1996): 1615.

23 Ibid.

24 A. Logmans et al.,"Ethical Dilemma: Should Doctors Reconstruct the Vaginal State," *British Medical Journal* 316 (February 7, 1998): 459.

25 Ibid., 460.

26 L. A. Kauffman, "220,000 Jesus Fans Can't Be Wrong: Praise the Lord, and Mammon," *The Nation* 259/9 (September 25, 1994): 306–10.

27 Dina Ezzat, "Islamic Law Drives Arab Women to Illegal Surgery to Save their Lives," *The Times* (London), June 16, 1996.

28 Judith Butler, "Variations on Sex and Gender: Beauvoir, Wittig and Foucault," *Feminism as Critique: Essays on the Politics of Gender in Late-Capitalist Societies*, ed. Seyla Benhabib and Drucilla Cornell (Cambridge: Polity Press, 1987), 140.

29 Ibid., 141.

30 Monique Wittig, "The Straight Mind," *The Straight Mind and Other Essays* (Boston: Beacon Press, 1992), 32.

31 Leigh Gilmore, "An Anatomy of Absence: Written on the Body, The Lesbian Body and Autobiography Without Names," *The Gay 90s: Disciplinary and Interdisciplinary Formations in Queer Studies*, ed. Thomas Foster, Carol Siegel, and Ellen E. Berry (New York: New York University Press, 1997), 225.

32 Ibid., 249 n. 2.

33 Butler, "Variations on Sex and Gender," 133.

34 Gilmore, "Anatomy of Absence," 235.

35 Ibid., 240.

36 Ibid., 246.

37 Ibid., 248.

CHAPTER FIVE

Wandering Wounds

It is better to be wounded than to be dead.
—St. Isaac of Syria[1]

When Miguel de Cervantes published what is today known as the first part of *Don Quijote de la Mancha* in 1605, he may have thought that his labor as chronicler of the wanderings of the man of La Mancha had come to an end. The 1605 version ends with burlesque sonnets that serve as epitaphs to the tombs of Don Quijote, Dulcinea del Toboso, Don Quijote's horse Rocinante, and Sancho Panza, supposedly taken from fragments of decaying parchments that the "author of the history" mentions were found in a leaden box and transcribed from gothic handwriting into legible, contemporary letters. The last paragraph of the book says that some diligent academic has also deciphered from those parchments the story of the third (and in 1605) as yet unwritten sally of Don Quijote, and that he intends to publish the tale. But the last six words of the text are a mistranscription from Ariosto's *Orlando Furioso* (canto 30, stanza 16), in Cervantes's Italian: "Forsi altro canterá con miglior plectro," or, correctly, in Italian, "Forse altri canterà con miglior plettro," or, "Some bard of defter quill may sing [it] some day."[2]

Because of this suggestion that some else might tell the story in the future, we cannot say whether Cervantes ever intended to write a sequel to the first part. What we can say is that the Ariosto quotation was sufficient to serve as an invitation to an imitator, the still-to-be-identified "Alonso Fernández de Avellaneda," who composed *The Second Volume of the Ingenious Gentleman Don Quijote of la Mancha*, published in 1614. This book was to influence strongly the literary world that Cervantes creates in the second part of the authentic *Don Quijote* (1615). In this text Don Quijote and Sancho Panza find that they are characters in a book—that they have, indeed, a virtual existence subject to the interpretations of their chroniclers and critics. This theme is nascent in the metaliterary aspects of the First Part, but it blossoms into a new way to tell stories in the Second, and some critics[3] have said that the intrusion of

Avellaneda's text into the textuality and history of Don Quijote provoked the author to make sure that everyone witnessed the demise of Don Quijote by the end of the 1615 book, and to insist that his Moorish historian Cide Hamete-Benengeli hang up his pen, unequivocally, at the end.

Cervantes's integration of multiple textualities and historical realities in the Second Part of *Don Quijote de la Mancha* are a crucial part of what makes a still-unsurpassed, radically innovative narrative experiment. But the Prologue, too, in an intensely concentrated way, has a great deal to teach about writing, reading, and relationship. Like many authors, Cervantes wrote the prologue late in the game, certainly after 1614 and the appearance of Avellaneda's sequel. We know this because Cervantes quotes Avellaneda's prologue in his own. Avellaneda had written that "Cervantes is as old as the castle of San Cervantes [a very old castle]," and "I say hand [instead of hands] because he admits he has only one; and since he talks so much about other people, we have to say of him that he is a soldier as old in years as he is young in bravado, and that he has more of a tongue than he has hands."[4] This is all in the way of not very good-natured competitive professional banter; it is certainly cruel, but some may have found it funny. Nevertheless, for Cervantes it is deadly serious. He says that he can tolerate the fact that Avellaneda has adulterated the itinerary of his literary creation, but that

> What I cannot help resenting is that he charges me with being old and one-handed, as if it had been in my power to hinder time's passage, or as if the loss of my hand had occurred in some tavern and not the grandest occasion the past or present has seen or the future can hope to see.[5]

Cervantes is referring to his participation in the Battle of Lepanto. He lost the use of his left hand in this important 1571 naval conflict, in which a fleet of combatants from several Christian nations defeated the Muslim (Ottoman) Turks near the modern Greek coastal town of Navpaktos. Lepanto was crucial because it put an end to threats of Turkish naval supremacy in the Mediterranean, and decisively stopped Muslim westward expansion. Having participated in the battle of Lepanto, and having been wounded there, is like having been on Omaha Beach on D-Day (for a North American) or in the siege of Stalingrad (for a Russian). Lepanto was a stand-off between two imperial powers, and its outcome had an effect throughout the know world.

Cervantes's pride in having taken part is quite strong:

> If my wounds have no beauty to the beholder's eye, they are, at least, honorable in the estimation of those who know where they were received. The soldier shows to greater advantage dead in battle than alive in flight, and so strongly is this my feeling that, if now it were proposed to do the impossible for me, I would rather have taken part in that mighty action than be free from my wounds this minute and not have been there. The wounds the soldier shows on his face and breast are

stars that direct others to the heaven of honor and the search for merited praise. It is to be observed, moreover, that one writes not with grey hairs but the understanding, which commonly improves with years.[6]

He mentions his service at Lepanto in a petition to the Crown in which he asks to be granted a bureaucratic job in the Americas: "Miguel de Cervantes Saavedra says that he has served Your Majesty for many years in the sea and land campaigns that have occurred over the last 22 years, particularly in the Naval Battle [Lepanto], where he received many wounds, among which was the loss of a hand from gunfire [a musket blast (*arcabuzazo*)]."[7] Cervantes never got a position in the New World, and his career and future in Spain were rarely reliable or secure. Most kinds of work were impossible for him, because he could not use his left hand at all. No one granted him a sinecure. And so he turned to writing, work he could do with his normally functioning hand.

The prologue to the foundational text of modern Western narrative insists on the relationship between the disabling wound, writing, and history. Cervantes participated in a battle whose effect was to confirm Christian European political and economic hegemony. Another effect of the battle was to mutilate the body of Cervantes, to severely injure his left hand. I do not wish to write that he "lost the use of his left hand." Although the expression "differently-abled" (as a substitute for "disabled") is less than euphonious, it is accurate when it comes to describing the effect on writing of Cervantes's injury. Avellaneda's sequel injures Cervantes's aesthetic sense, and it wounds his pride, too. But Cervantes in the Prologue and throughout the 1615 *Quijote* emphasizes again and again the relationship between the body of the writer and the kind of text an author produces. A disabled, wounded body makes possible a kind of text that another kind of body cannot make. When a body broken in the service of Empire—wounded but not killed—takes up a pen or taps a keyboard, history moves into literature in a very specific way. The wound finds its way onto the page, and the fictions of dominance and mastery come undone.

There is no quick fix or miraculous healing of this kind of wound, and it cannot be said that writing works any redemptive magic. One effect of the unsought wound, though, is evident in early scene from the first part (1605) of *Don Quijote*. Just after the story is interrupted by the loss and then discovery of the manuscript it is allegedly based on, Don Quijote enters into hand-to-hand combat with an infuriated man of Biscay. The Biscayan deals him a terrific blow with his sword, but Don Quijote's life is spared.

> But that good fortune which reserved him for greater things turned aside the sword of his adversary so that, though it smote him upon the left shoulder, it did him no more harm than to strip all that side of his armor, carrying away a great part of his helmet with half of his ear.[8]

Don Quijote manages to level the Biscayan, and then removes himself from the battle. His squire Sancho Panza is alarmed, though:

> "What I beg of your worship is to take care of your wound, because a great deal of blood is flowing from that ear, and I have here some bandages and a little white ointment in the saddlebags."[9]

But Don Quijote cannot resist a reference to chivalric legend:

> "All that might well be dispensed with," said Don Quijote, "if I had remembered to make a vial of the balm of Fierabrás, for time and medicine are saved by a single drop."[10]

Don Quijote is alluding to the story of a Saracen giant named Fierabrás, who, as it is told in the legends of the Twelve Peers, stole from Rome the miraculous liquid with which the body of Jesus had been embalmed, which instantly healed wounds.[11] In the Christian West, the wounded body par excellence is that of Jesus Christ. In a chemically literalized reading of I Peter 2:24, "by his wounds you have been healed," the ointments in which the body of Christ steeped for three days have a concentrated power to transfer the resurrection to anybody's wounds. Sancho sees the money-making potential of this, since Don Quijote claims to have a recipe for making a generic version of the balm from cheap ingredients, but in the end the two must admit that they have none of this wonderful substance, and Don Quijote interrupts their reveries of pharmacological good fortune by saying,

> "For the present let us see to the dressing, for my ear pains me more than I could wish." Sancho took out some bandages and ointments from the saddlebags.[12]

As it turns out, Don Quijote's wound itself sanctifies and expands the narrative in ways that the marvelous balm of Fierabrás could never achieve. Because there is no magic cure, the wound must be integrated into the writing, and into the relationship between Don Quijote and Sancho. Cervantes's achievement and innovation in both parts of *Don Quijote* is to make embodied, discursive *relationship* both the means and the end of the story. Sancho has to touch Don Quijote's bleeding, banged-up ear, to clean it, salve it, bandage it. It will never be as good as new. It will never heal properly; the wound will leave scars. But the injury inscribed on the body testifies to a moment in which one human being sought the help of another, in which a human being saw another in need and made a necessary attempt to alleviate pain, even in the knowledge that he could not effect a perfect cure, or erase the bodily traces of the wound.

Cervantes tells the reader in the Prologue to the second part (1615) that some people, "those who know where they were received," find them "honorable."[13] But it is important to point out that neither Cervantes nor Don Quijote desires to be wounded. Neither seeks injury. Masochism is not at play here. What may be revealed here is an educative process, in which it is learned that being in combat can easily lead to being physically wounded—that fighting for an idea, or ideal (or intellection) has corporeal effects. This seemingly obvious insight is probably the most overlooked fact in the history of conquest in the West. People kill and are killed, wound and are wounded in wars. The effect that this wounding has on persons who are not self-destructive or bloodthirsty is paradoxically to make them vulnerable to healing and relationship, to dialogue and to narrative impulses. "It is better to be wounded than to be dead" because if you are wounded there is a chance that your battered body will tell a new kind of story, in a new way. An unwillingly opened body tells stories differently from an unopened body.

Don Quijote and Sancho serve as a model narrative pair for many different stories that come after theirs, some of which do not in any way transmit the spirit of vulnerable relationship that accompanies the two Spaniards. Recent cases might include the "buddy" narratives of violence and retribution that are at the present an unavoidable and profitable Hollywood genre. But these homosocial rituals of fascist monologism have little in common with a quixotic relationship. Interestingly, the buddies in these films are often policemen or soldiers. They suffer many wounds and bleed copiously, but are miraculously unaffected in their physical prowess by the blows they take.

It is interesting to compare these films with texts that are their antecedents in popular culture. In terms of the buddy movie, it is important to acknowledge the influence of Sir Arthur Conan Doyle's Sherlock Holmes stories. Sherlock Holmes and his assistant and chronicler Dr. Watson form part of a trajectory that moves through writers like Dashiell Hammett into *film noir* and then mutates distantly into the bludgeoning simplicity of the present-day buddy-blockbuster. But Sherlock Holmes and Dr. Watson have something in common with the relationship at the beginning of modern narrative, too. Like Don Quijote, Holmes is tall, thin, eccentric, often lost in reading and reverie, sometimes bizarrely ascetic; Watson, like Sancho, moves slowly, advocates caution and practicalities, requires creature comforts. Both Sancho and Watson are battlefield medics. Don Quijote and Holmes depend on Sancho and Watson for their narrative existence; without their dialogues, there is no story. The innovation in Conan Doyle's texts is that the functions of narrator and companion are condensed into one discursive role—Watson's—rather than into two or more (as in the case of *Don Quijote*, in which Cervantes and narrative voices derivative of his record the story, and Sancho, who can neither read nor write, is companion).

The whole corpus of Conan Doyle's forty years of writing Holmes stories is introduced in the first paragraphs of the first tale, the novel *A Study in Scarlet* (1887) under the rubric "Being a Reprint from the Reminiscences of John H. Watson, M.D., Late of the Army Medical Department."[14] Like *Don Quijote*, the stories are rooted in a documentary pretense—excerpted, supposedly, from a pre-existing archive. The subtitle to the first chapter is "Mr. Sherlock Holmes." But the first pages of the book are all about Watson. In the first person, from the first words, "Mr. Sherlock Holmes" is a chapter about Watson, with detailed paragraphs on his history as a soldier and doctor as part of the imperial British Army's expeditions to subdue Afghanistan.

Chiefly, we learn of a painful incident on the battlefield: "The campaign brought honours and promotion to many, but for me it had nothing but misfortune and disaster."[15] In this Watson is like Cervantes. "Honours and promotion" do not follow his participation in a crucial imperial battle. Of course, the Spanish and other European Christians won the battle of Lepanto and the British Empire lost terribly "at the fatal battle of Maiwand."[16] For Watson, personally, there was trouble:

> There [at Maiwand] I was struck on the shoulder by a Jezail bullet, which shattered the bone and grazed the subclavian artery. I should have fallen to the hands of the murderous Ghazis had it not been for the devotion and courage shown by Murray, my orderly, who threw me across a pack-horse, and succeeded in bringing me safely to the British lines.[17]

Not only is Watson wounded, but during his time of convalescence he becomes sick for months with enteric fever, and is finally sent home to England with a tiny pension, his "health irretrievably ruined."[18]

Watson meets an old acquaintance who knows of an eccentric fellow who is looking for a roommate—and Watson is impecunious enough that he needs to share lodgings. Off they go to the chemical laboratory to meet this strange man. They find Holmes just having invented a new test for the detection of blood stains. (Like Celestina before him, Holmes is at work brewing up stories in his lab; the *pharmakon* appears here, as it must at the invention of a new kind of narrative.[19]) Watson's friend brings the two men together, and Holmes's first words at the moment of meeting are:

> "How are you?" he said cordially, gripping my hand with a strength for which I should hardly have given him credit. "You have been in Afghanistan, I perceive."[20]

Watson is astonished. How did Holmes know? He does not explain to Watson until after the two have moved in together, when Holmes delineates the train of thought that led him to know that Watson had come from Afghanistan:

> I knew you came from Afghanistan. From long habit the train of thoughts ran so swiftly through my mind that I arrived at the conclusion without being conscious of intermediate steps. There were such steps, however. The train of reasoning ran, "Here is a gentleman of a medical type, but with the air of a military man. Clearly an army doctor, then. He has just come from the tropics, for his face is dark, and that is not the natural tint of his skin, for his wrists are fair. He has undergone hardship and sickness, as his haggard face says clearly. His left arm has been

injured. He holds it in a stiff and unnatural manner. Where in the tropics could an English army doctor have seen much hardship and got his arm wounded? Clearly in Afghanistan."[21]

Among the other observations, Holmes specifically notes, "His left arm has been injured. He holds it in a stiff and unnatural manner." The first deduction of the great sleuth—introduced, but not explained, before the hemoglobin test—is that Watson is an English army doctor whose left arm was wounded in Afghanistan. Watson meets Holmes only because of this wound. The Sherlock Holmes stories exist in narrative only because Watson was wounded in a war he had entered as a healer (as an army surgeon), in Afghanistan, helping a war effort that sought to uphold the dominance of the British Empire in a very distant Muslim land. Watson has in common with Cervantes and Don Quijote that his left arm and shoulder are wounded and disabled and that this wound leads him into a discursive relationship that has far-reaching consequences for narrative.

The military events to which Watson alludes are not distant from the date of the publication of *A Study in Scarlet* (1887). He immediately embodies the traumas of the British colonial enterprise. Cervantes writes the Prologue to the Second Part of *Don Quijote* almost thirty-five years after the Battle of Lepanto. What the two wounded old soldiers have in common is that the time of their writing is one in which the Empires they fought for are just at the moment of tipping into irreversible decline. They are beginning to inscribe imperial error.

In Watson's case, this error is physically and textually embodied. As it turns out, Watson often makes chronological errors in his recordings of his and Holmes's adventures. "It is all of a piece with his remarkable vagueness on other matters... His own name, for example. Like A.A. Milne's raindrops 'Both of him had different names: / one was John and one was James.'"[22] (Some critique these kinds of inconsistencies in *Don Quijote* for Cervantes, too. Donkeys disappear, chapter headings have nothing to do with their content, etc.) Watson's wound also errs: in *The Noble Bachelor*, it is "in one of my limbs." *The Sign of Four* finds him "nursing my wounded leg. I had had a Jezail bullet through it some time before."[23] And of course there is his first mention of the wound, where he places it in his left shoulder. While the wound wanders, its cause does not—"the Jezail bullet" is what did the damage, even if the location wanders. Yet in that first encounter with Holmes, the detective is entirely specific about the site of the wound: "His left arm has been injured." It is not crucial or possible to diagnose and heal the wound. What does matter is to witness it, and to provide room (or rooms, as Holmes did) in which the wound may write itself out, if it can or would, in contact with another body.

Watson expresses his surprise at Holmes's deductive powers by comparing him to "Edgar Allan Poe's Dupin."[24] But Holmes does not care for the comparison:

"No doubt you think that you are complimenting me in comparing me to Dupin," he observed. "Now, in my opinion, Dupin was a very inferior fellow. That trick of breaking in on his friends' thoughts with an apropos remark after a quarter of an hour's silence is really very showy and superficial. He had some analytical genius, no doubt; but he was by no means such a phenomenon as Poe appeared to imagine."[25]

Like Don Quijote and Sancho, Sherlock and Watson compete with other literary figures as if they were historical.

What is a detective, or an investigator, after all? Frequently it is someone who tries to find out the secrets of another, but who is ignorant of what his own secrets might be. But of course, the unconscious motivation is always to discover and understand something for and about oneself. Dupin's failure for Holmes may be that he will not get his hands dirty. The clearest thematic root of this might be the childhood sexual investigations that provide a foundation for the detective story.[26] But behind even those primordial explorations there is a deeper desire, not just for factual knowledge, but for existential confirmation. Narrative that is something other than the mechanical repetition of received notions can come into writing when I find that the hand with which I wish to probe your wound is itself wounded (John 20:24–29). This wound wanders back and forth through time and space, from you to me and back again. Hysteria, or "wandering womb," was dubbed a conversion neurosis by the early psychoanalysts. In hysteria bodies communicate what language cannot. Hysteria manifests a paralyzed and paralyzing femininity until a "talking cure" makes truth-telling and a new kind of gendered embodiment possible. The "wandering wound" of imperial war-making hurts, too. It too requires a new inscription of masculinity, and certainly a new poetics of the vulnerable. There may be a sadistic pleasure in poking into other people's wounds. But probing them sometimes also happens to relieve doubt: are you really here? Are you, really? Am I? Moving beyond this narcissistic inquiry into dialogue, waiting, and witness can help show that a wound can be proof that the body is the source of the story. Wounded veterans of foreign wars frequently learn that killing in order to get power unmakes history.

Notes

1　Also known as St. Isaac of Nineveh (the site of the ancient city is, of course, in present-day Iraq).

2　Miguel de Cervantes, *The Ingenious Gentleman Don Quijote of La Mancha*, Part II, *Don Quijote: A Norton Critical Edition*, ed. Joseph R. Jones and Kenneth Douglas (New York: W. W. Norton, 1981), 433.

3　See, for example, Stephen Gilman, "The Apocryphal Quijote," *Don Quijote: A Norton Critical Edition*, ed. Jones and Douglas, 994–1002.

4　Cervantes, *The Ingenious Gentleman Don Quijote of La Mancha*, Part II, 535.

5 Ibid., 415.

6 Ibid.

7 Manuel Durán, "Cervantes' Harassed and Vagabond Life," *Don Quijote: A Norton Critical Edition*, ed. Jones and Douglas, 837–38.

8 Cervantes, *The Ingenious Gentleman Don Quijote of La Mancha*, Part I, 68.

9 Ibid., 70.

10 Ibid.

11 Ibid., n. 4.

12 Ibid., 71.

13 Cervantes, *The Ingenious Gentleman Don Quijote of La Mancha*, Part II, 415.

14 Sir Arthur Conan Doyle, *A Study in Scarlet, The Complete Sherlock Holmes*, vol. I (New York: Doubleday, 1922), 15.

15 Ibid.

16 Ibid.

17 Ibid.

18 Ibid.

19 See, for instance, Roberto González Echevarría's essay on Celestina in *Celestina's Brood*. Of course, for a discussion on the significance of the word *pharmakon* see Barbara Johnson's translation of Jacques Derrida's *Dissemination*, specifically the section, "Plato's Pharmacy" (Chicago: University of Chicago Press, 1981).

20 Conan Doyle, *A Study in Scarlet*, 17–18.

21 Ibid., 24.

22 Michael Hardwick, *The Sherlock Holmes Companion* (New York: Doubleday, 1963), 198.

23 Ibid., 198–99.

24 Conan Doyle, *A Study in Scarlet*, 24.

25 Ibid.

26 See Marie Bonaparte's psychoanalytic study, "The Murders in Rue Morgue," *Psychoanalytic Quarterly* 4 (1935).

CHAPTER SIX

Language Butcher Dupes Dupin

The Murders in the Rue Morgue[1] are committed by an orangutan who wants to play barber but who ends up instead cast in the role of barbarian. His story goes like this: a sailor and a companion capture the orangutan on a voyage to Borneo. The sailor's companion dies, and the sailor brings the orangutan back to Paris in order to sell it.

Very early one morning, while it is still dark, the sailor returns home from a party. He finds that the orangutan has broken out of the closet in which it has been locked up, and now is sitting in front of a mirror, fully lathered, with a razor, and is "attempting the operation of shaving, in which it had no doubt previously watched its master through the key-hole of the closet" (407). The sailor grabs the whip he customarily uses to subdue the orangutan, but the animal flees out into the streets of the metropolis, with the razor still in hand. At this very late or very early hour, the animal finds an apartment where somebody is still up—there is a light on in the fourth story apartment above. The orangutan clambers up a lightning rod and enters through an open window.

Inside, a certain Madame L'Espanaye and her daughter are, inexplicably, "arranging some papers" (408) in an iron chest. Unfortunately, this late-night reading will have disastrous consequences for their own coiffure. The orangutan seizes Mme. L'Espanaye by the hair, and "was flourishing the razor about her face, in imitation of the motions of a barber" (408). Confronted with the exigencies of this beauty treatment, the daughter faints. The mother, misunderstanding the orangutan's cosmetological intentions, screams and struggles, infuriating it; in a moment the razor has slit her throat. Now enraged, the orangutan strangles the unconscious daughter. All along, the sailor, not a bad climber himself, has been perched outside on the lightning rod, watching the gruesome events through the window. On seeing the face of its captor, the orangutan becomes filled with fear, and so tries to hide the body of the daughter by shoving it up the chimney. It flings the mother out the window as the sailor slinks away.

It is the job of Poe's detective, Dupin, to figure out that all of this has occurred. The only evidence the police have is the bodies and the reports of witnesses who have heard but not seen anything. By picking up on evidence that the police have missed, and by analyzing the gaps, slips, and guesses in the witnesses' state-ments, Dupin solves the mystery. The sailor eventually recovers the orangutan and makes a pretty penny by selling it to the zoo.

Many critics have observed that this is a murder mystery with no motive and no one to blame. But two women are dead, and the orangutan must spend the rest of its (its sex is not specified) life behind bars, far from home. The text certainly punishes the women and the barbering ape. The narrative economy makes the women and the orangutan kin, but what blood could entities so foreign to each other have in common?

The first reports that Dupin reads of the murders are in the "Gazette de Tribuneaux." Twelve people give statements about the crime; six of them are ear-witnesses. These include the local gendarme and five other neighborhood men who ascended the stairs of the L'Espanaye home to try to investigate the source of the blood-curdling screams. All six of the men depose that they heard two voices in contention, but the witnesses disagree about the provenance of those voices. The first witness, the gendarme, heard a gruff Frenchman saying *sacré* and *diable*. The second voice was shrill. He was not sure of its gender. He could not make out what it said, but believed the language it spoke to be Spanish. Henri Duval, the next witness, another Frenchman, is also unsure of the gender of the shrill voice but thinks it spoke in Italian. However, he does not know Italian. After him, a Dutch restaurateur, who does not speak French, tells through an interpreter that the shrill voice was a man—a Frenchman. An English tailor says that the shrill voice was loud, possibly female, and German. But the tailor does not understand German. There is a Spanish undertaker named Alfonso Garcio who lives in the Rue Morgue. He too heard the voices. The shrill one was that of an Englishman—Garcio doesn't understand English, but judges by the intonation. Finally, an Italian confectioner says that the shrill voice is Russian. But he has "never conversed with a native of Russia" (390).

Dupin does not miss the obvious point here, which is

> how strangely unusual must that voice have really been, about which testimony such as this *could* have been elicited!—in whose *tones*, even, denizens of the five great divisions of Europe could recognize nothing familiar! You will say that it might have been the voice of an Asiatic—of an African. Neither Asiatics nor Africans abound in Paris! (396; emphasis added)

What Dupin insists on is that "No words—no sounds resembling words—were by any witness mentioned as distinguishable."

What is a "sound resembling a word?" Perhaps "babble." The onomatopoetic root of this word connects with both 'Babel' and 'barbarian.' Each witness spoke of the shrill voice "as that *of a foreigner*. Each is sure that it was not the voice of one of is own countrymen" (395). The incomprehensible speech is heard as that of a barbarian: someone uncivilized and brutal who most certainly does not speak my language. In the absence of evidence, I blame the one I cannot understand, not only because he does not speak my language, but because I cannot speak his.

The witnesses let their ignorance guide them and produce their assumptions. They project their own meaning—specific, national meaning—upon that which they find unintelligible. The difference between them and Dupin is that Dupin is willing to learn from the knowledge that neither he nor anyone else knows what language, if any, the voice used. The witnesses, confronted with difference, refer to a priori categories as a way of fixing and naming that difference, and assuaging their anxiety before it. They will limit and stop the echo of difference—but Dupin is willing to learn from it, at least consciously.

Of course the sad part of this story, like most other murder mysteries, is that the investigator only answers the question "Who done it?"—he does not stop the murder from happening in the first place. The detective's demonstrations of analytical mastery are nourished by corpses. Someone's bodies are always being sacrificed so that he may learn and teach. In this case, typically, these are women's bodies. But Poe, even though he is, with *The Murders in the Rue Morgue*, the inventor of the detective story, is not the first fiction writer to fuel his narrative with dead women. It is not my intention here to try to explain the consumption of women's bodies by Western narrative; that habit has already been amply theorized.[2] But in Poe's case, and in the specific case of the detective story, Marie Bonaparte's 1935 analysis in *Psychoanalytic Quarterly* is still convincing: that the pleasure that readers derive from mystery stories comes from "the fact that the researches conducted by the detective reproduce, by displacement onto subjects of a quite different nature, our infantile investigations into matters of sex,"[3] and that in "these infantile observations" "the child invariably interprets what he has seen or heard as an act of violence and cruelty of which the woman is the victim. This conception, called by Freud the *sadistic conception of coitus*, is found in analysis to be present in the unconscious of every individual."[4] Bonaparte's Freudian theory explains the penchant of detective fiction for dead female or feminized bodies. (It might also explain the pleasures and terrors of psychoanalysis itself for both analyst and analysand, and provides a clue for the meaning of the female body as figure in psychoanalytic writing.)

Poe adds another layer to the problem by introducing the element of language into the primal scene. Bonaparte alludes to this, too, in her explanation of the perspicacity of the young child's sexual investigations:

> It is difficult for us, with our adult processes of thought, to form any conception of the workings of instinct, intelligence, and observation in the child of one and a half years. Certain it is that children of that age are already capable of notable achievements such as learning to talk. Connecting a given sound with the representation of an object, for instance, is a feat which no animal, however intelligent, has ever succeeded in imitating.[5]

Bonaparte and Freud state that little children may mistake parental cries of pleasure for those of pain, and that the limitations of their knowledge and experience make it impossible for them to hear it any other way. A child cannot adopt a wait-and-see attitude before such a crucial enigma, and so projects what it is sure of into the vacuum of what completely escapes its analytical powers. And so the child errs, perhaps—as Bonaparte reminds us, sometimes cries of pain are just cries of pain. In any case, the child may misinterpret the sounds it hears. In this respect, the child is like the auricular witnesses to the murders in the Rue Morgue, who feel compelled to specify, in the absence of certainty, the *national origin* of the sounds they hear. Poe's witnesses seem to have more difficulty with gender than the child does, though. Three of the witnesses are unsure as to whether the shrill voice belongs to a man or a woman. What happens behind the closed doors of the apartment confounds gender distinctions. Oddly enough, the witnesses are able to name the national language of the shrieker. Gender collapses, but nationalized linguistic distinctions do not. One of the "five great divisions of Europe" in particular recurs with effect in the story, in a way that may help us understand Poe's conception of the mystery of foreign tongues and bodies.

We know that Madame L'Espanaye and her daughter are Frenchwomen, but the neighbors find them suspicious because they have money, but never go out; further, the rumor has circulated that they are fortunetellers. Thus the neighbors think that the L'Espanayes know something that they, the neighbors, do not. Their neighbors do not understand them. Is there a secret embedded in their secretive characters? If we boil them down to their linguistic essence, we can follow Poe's biographer, Kenneth Silverman, who points out that the name "L'Espanaye" "... contains Poe's initials twice and also nearly makes *Allan* (Poe's middle name)."[6] Under such stimulus it seems necessary to point out what is probably obvious already, which is that without any anagrammatic work at all it is possible to read the word "España" in the middle of the murdered women's last name. The first witness who heard the two voices, the gendarme, says that he "could distinguish some words of the former, which was that of a Frenchman. Was positive that it was not a woman's voice. Could distinguish the words 'sacre' and 'diable'" (388). The policeman, a Frenchman, is certain of the gender, nationality, and language of that which is like him. When he speaks of the dubious second voice, he states that "the shrill voice was that of a foreigner. Could not be sure if it was a man or a woman. Could not make out what was said, but believed the language to be Spanish" (388). The voice of the French lawman, confronted with uncertainty, is very specific in its observations: he stipulates that the second voice was that of a foreigner, and that this foreigner of confounded gender was speaking Spanish. The testimony sets up an opposition between a familiar, masculine, French-speaker, and a foreign, feminized (because not assuredly masculine) Spanish-speaker. The testimony of the gendarme is crucial in several respects. It is the voice of the law, handing down the most official version of the story. Also, the gendarme's is the first linguistic diagnosis. And finally, it establishes a French/Spanish opposition that makes of Spanish the foreign tongue par excellence.

As I mentioned earlier, another Frenchman testifies, but he thinks that the shrill voice "was that of an Italian. Was certain that it was not French. Could not be sure that it was a man's voice. It might have been a woman's. Was not acquainted with the Italian language" (388). Again we have the insistence on the foreignness of the voice, and on its confusing gender. This witness's testimony is mainly interesting because of the way that, by way of a slip Poe makes in the writing of the tale, it reinforces the emphasis on Spanish as the most foreign of tongues.

Later in the story when Dupin is analyzing all of the testimony on the languages spoken behind closed doors, he summarizes by saying that "Each [witness] likens it—not to the voice of an individual of any nation with whose language he is conversant—but the converse." Such a cacophonous use of "conversant" and "converse" is a strange event in itself. Even odder is what comes next. Dupin says that "the Frenchman [the gendarme] supposes it the voice of a Spaniard and 'might have distinguished some words had he been acquainted with the Spanish'" (395). But at no time does the gendarme use these words—they are from the second Frenchman's testimony, not the gendarme's. The gendarme says "Could not make out what was said, but believed the language to be Spanish" (388). The gendarme is unique in the list of witnesses because he is the only one who never specifies an ignorance of the tongue he names. When Poe uses the verb "acquainted," he is conflating the testimony of the two Frenchmen, and letting Dupin miss a loophole in the gendarme's testimony. Spanish eludes his detective mastery. Spanish marks the spot of uncertainty in the text.

Spain is a problem for Poe. In the Rue Morgue he has to butcher Spanish three times, once in the person of Madame L'Espanaye, once in that of her dead daughter, and once with a slip of the narratological knife in the error Dupin makes when he mixes up the linguistic testimony. Furthermore, it is plausible to suggest that the Rue Morgue gets its name from the business of the one Spaniard mentioned in the text, Alfonso Garcio, who, as we learned earlier, is an under-taker. The "o" at the end of Garcio, normally Garcia, is another form of butchery, and one that promotes gender confusion in its unexplained manipulations of "o" and "a," the vowels that most frequently determine the gender of nouns in Spanish.[7] Spain is deadly and strange in others of his tales, as well. In *The Cask of Amontillado* the Italian Fortunato's fondness for Spanish wine enables his murderer to chain him up and immure him. *The Pit and the Pendulum* credits the Spanish Inquisition with the invention of the most celebrated torture chamber in fiction, and firmly establishes, in its last lines, a French = Life, Spanish = Death opposition: "An outstretched arm caught my own as I fell, fainting, into the abyss. It was that of General Lasalle. The French army had entered Toledo. The Inquisition was in the hands of its enemies."[8] French is the language of the known and safe, Spanish of the unknown and threatening, in Poe's tales.

If the detective story exists to maintain the pleasures of infantile sexual investigations, it also works to control the anxieties that those investigations precipitated. Its heroes are great sleuths whose analytical powers satisfactorily resolve unwelcome doubts, and who provide consoling certainties and solutions. The detective knows what we want, which is to know the unknown. He saves us, we think, from the fate of the orangutan, which is trying to learn, but which is punished because it is unable either to understand or to be understood. It imitates, but cannot communicate. Despite our efforts at detection, the desires of others will always be at least partly a mystery to us. The sounds we hear but do not understand are those of a pleasure to which we have not yet gained access; as Bonaparte says, at age one-and-a-half or so we are just beginning to learn a language of desire that we will spend all of our lives trying not to butcher. For Poe, in *The Murders in the Rue Morgue*, Spanish is evidence of the unintelligible meaning of the other, a language the other cannot understand, either. Because the inability to understand is unbearable to the orangutan, it tries to kill it off in the feminized forms of Madame and Mademoiselle L'Espanaye, in whose name Spain and France, the foreign and the familiar, are inseparable and mutually disruptive. But the inability to master everything returns to haunt the narrative in the form of a factual and narratological slip. Bodies suffer and die. Much is sacrificed to further the investigations, which always occur too late. The explanations are insufficient and flawed. Dupin, the great and primordial investigator, errs on a crucial point. How can we be sure that he was right about the rest?

Notes

1 Edgar Allan Poe, *The Murders in the Rue Morgue: Tales of Mystery and Imagination* (London: J. M. Dent & Sons, 1912). All internal citations refer to this edition.

2 For an elaboration of a related argument see Teresa de Lauretis's "Desire in Narrative."

3 Bonaparte, "Murders in Rue Morgue," 292.

4 Ibid., 281.

5 Ibid., 279.

6 Kenneth Silverman, *Edgar A. Poe: Mournful and Never-ending Remembrance* (New York: HarperCollins, 1991), 173.

7 A comparison with Roland Barthes' *S/Z* might be useful here. In that reading of Balzac's short story "Sarrazine" Barthes analyzes the orthographic irregularities in the protagonist's name specifically in reference to the effect that spelling has on the rhetorics of gender and power (Roland Barthes, *S/Z: An Essay*, trans. Richard Miller [New York: Hill and Wang, 1974]).

8 Edgar Allan Poe, *The Pit and the Pendulum, The Works of Edgar Allan Poe*, vol. II (New York: P. F. Collier & Sons, 1904), 256.

Entremes:
"Nobody Expects the Spanish Inquisition"

Velásquez paints himself into the picture in *Las Meninas*. His position is like that of a U.S. Spanish professor commenting on the place of Spain in the U.S. academic imaginary. Velásquez was smart enough to know that, painted in or not, he was part of the picture he was creating, and part of the scene that he was commenting on. Thus he avoided, somewhat, the dangers of projection—that is, of attributing to others his own thoughts and emotions. It seems to me that this is a risk of trying to analyze what other parts of the academy think of what we, professors and students of Spanish and Latin American texts and cultures, are doing. I do not know what they think of me and my work. What I have to contribute is anecdotal and experiential: that is to say, direct and unarguable, but hard to quantify.

When people outside of Hispanism ask me what I teach, I have to tell them, "Cervantes, you know, *Don Quijote*," because the terms Golden Age or Early Modern Spain really do not connote anything to them. I say Spain, you say "Don Quijote," is pretty much the inevitable progress of the free association. And the only thing most people know about Don Quijote is the windmills, or Picasso's simple sketch, or Dulcinea, or the song "The Impossible Dream," which of course has nothing to do with Don Quijote at all. In my experience, this is a real conversation killer. (In fact the only answer more deadly is my other one: "I teach Women's and Gender Studies.") The only way out is the Inquisition. The Spanish Inquisition is second on the list of most likely free associations. People know less about the Inquisition than they do about Don Quijote, yet they frequently express deeply held feelings and ideas about it. But their knowledge comes from fiction; at best Poe, perhaps; at worst Monty Python.

Monty Python's skit presents a troupe of pointlessly serious, inept cardinals oozing with an uncontrollable sadism that is entirely thwarted by the torture devices at their disposal—a rack for draining dishes; some soft pillows, meant to poke the accused into a confession of guilt; and finally the machine of last resort, a large "comfy chair," in which the victim is forced to sit until lunchtime with only a coffee break half way through the torture to ease her agonies.

Sometimes I fear that this is how professors in other language and literature departments see Spanish professors—particularly colleagues in departments of "Literatures in English," which in recent cases have begun to feature *Don Quixote*, as if Cervantes wrote in English, the way Jesus is supposed to have spoken English, since that is the language of the King James Version of the Bible. If they do see us this way, I think it tells us something about the situations of English and Spanish, that star-crossed pair, in the U.S. academy, and where the disciplines might be headed in the future.

First, and most obviously, the cardinals of the Inquisition in the skit are played by English actors with outrageously overstated English accents. They are Englishmen in Spanish drag. They are using images of Spain to critique England the way that drag queens use the performance of femininity to critique masculinity (and of course drag was one of the Python group's favorite comedic devices). What this provides for us now is an overview of the symptoms of panic and anxiety that the rise of Spanish in terms of bureaucratic power and presence in the U.S. academy is beginning to produce in other disciplines. The Python skit pitches a twisted battle between English and Spanish. The binary opposition is set—French, German, and Italian are nowhere to be seen. The powerful languages of high culture have been pushed off the stage, and instead we come again to a face-off between Queen Elizabeth and Philip the Second. As on the eve of the Armada's voyage, the academic high seas are to be dominated by either English or Spanish—only this time, there is a markedly better weather forecast for the Spanish fleet. Significantly, the performance of Spain causes a breakdown in language production. The chief cardinal, "Ximenez," cannot get his lines right:

> NOBODY expects the Spanish Inquisition! Our chief weapon is surprise... surprise and fear... fear and surprise... Our two weapons are fear and surprise... and ruthless efficiency... Our three weapons are fear, surprise, and ruthless efficiency... and an almost fanatical devotion to the Pope... Our four... no... Amongst our weapons... Amongst our weaponry... are such elements as fear, surprise... I'll come in again.[1]

The mere mention of Spain literally stops English syntax in its tracks. This disturbance or interruption can be read as an eruption of a repressed historical memory. There really was a time when Spain was more powerful than England, on land and sea. But in a long, long spiral, Spain lost its Empire. The lesson of this is that it is not only ancient empires that come to an end in broken rock. Modern empires can fall, too. Nebrija was right when he said that "language is the girlfriend [the *compañera*] of empire."[2] Language, economics, and ideology operate together. The rise of Spanish in the U.S. academy is disrupting the dominance of English, an unwelcome reminder, to some, that what goes up must come down.

It is necessary to mention, however, that what applies in the English/Spanish binary does not necessarily apply outside it. Not long ago I taught an introductory theory course for Comparative literature graduate students. There were students from Serbia, China, Taiwan, Spain, Puerto Rico; U.S. Latinas and African American women were represented, there was a white man from the U.S. suburbs who had spent years in the Czech republic, a woman who had taught world literature in a public school in the Bronx, someone who was into feminism and Anglo-North American modernism. It may not be novel, but it must be said that these students, who were all multilingual, who either came from countries other than the U.S. or had spent significant time out of the country, were insistent on the fact that English is today's lingua franca, if that is not mixing etymologies too much. To get to where the power is, you still have to speak English.

Of course, my preceding sentence only reiterates an earlier point. The stylistically unhappy phrase, "English is today's lingua franca," highlights the ways that the imperial dominance of languages waxes and wanes. This is especially true in systems that operate solely on the basis of vertical power structures. Here I have recourse to Cervantes's *Colloquy of the Dogs*. Camacha is a witch who, supposedly, changed the newborn children of her colleague La Montiela into the dogs who themselves narrate the story. On her deathbed, Camacha reassures their mother that the dogs:

> Volverán en su forma verdadera
> Cuando vieren con presta diligencia
> Derribar los soberbios levantados
> Y alzar a los humildes abatidos
> Por poderosa mano para hacerlo.[3]

> (They will return to their true form
> when they see with ready power
> the casting down of the high and proud
> and the lifting up of the downtrodden lowly ones
> by a hand mighty to do it)

The mighty will be cast down, and the lowly lifted up, and then the dogs (who were victims of professional jealousy—Camacha turned them into animals because she envied their mother's expertise) will return to their "true form." In the context of Spain and the U.S. academic imaginary, this text is particularly apt. Spanish departments are on the verge of being lifted to new heights in the academic hierarchy—but not without risk, and certainly with no guarantees. Where there is a verge, as we now know, there is also the possibility of a nervous breakdown—in this case, precipitated by unforeseen pedagogical challenges, many new students, budget shortfalls, cultural triumphalism both within and without Hispanism, and other impediments.

The prophecy that the dogs quote, like Velásquez's painting or the Python skit, contains its own caution. Casting down the high and lifting up the low only perpetuates a vertical structure of dominance. It does not do anything to dismantle the "power-over" model of human or academic relations that still, obviously, pertains in the university. One of the things that yesterday's losers can bring to the challenge of being today's winners is an analytical position that makes possible the creation of new models for pedagogy, cooperation, even by-laws and bureaucracy. People who study Spanish literature and culture already know, or ought to, that the Inquisitorial, Imperial model does not work. Writers like Cervantes provide us with constant reminders that it is possible to break with formula, and to read and write our way into a different kind of political and pedagogical reality.

Notes

1 Monty Python, "The Spanish Inquisition," cited online at http://peoplecsail.mit.edu/paulfitz/spanish/script.html.
2 See the Prologue to Antonio de Nebrija's *Gramática de la lengua castellana* (Madrid: Ediciones de Cultura Hispánica, 1992).
3 Miguel de Cervantes, *Coloquio de los perros, Novelas ejemplares*, vol. 3, ed. Juan Bautista Avalle-Arce (Madrid: Castalia, 1985), 294.

CHAPTER SEVEN

"My Hispanism Was Only a Symptom"

The Wolf-Man came to Freud in February of 1910 and stayed until June, 1914; his last session was the day after the assassination of the Archduke Franz Ferdinand in Sarajevo that precipitated the First World War. After he lost his home and fortune in the Russian revolution, the Wolf-Man returned to Freud for a brief analysis in 1919. From 1919 through 1938 he lived more or less (by his own account) symptom-free in Vienna with his wife, Therese. In March, 1938, after the Anschluss of Austria with Nazi Germany, his wife killed herself, and he declined into poor mental health. At that time the psychoanalyst Muriel Gardiner, the person who later encouraged him to write his autobiography,[1] secured visas for him to leave Vienna so that he could be analyzed by Ruth Mack Brunswick in Paris and London. He went back to Vienna in 1939 and rode out the Second World War and the Russian occupation there. He contributed now and then to psychoanalytic publications until his death at the age of 92.

He began writing his memoirs at age 83, that is, in 1970. The text is informed by Freud's case history "From the History of an Infantile Neurosis." Freud wrote his version down in winter 1914–15; because of the First World War, it was not published until 1918;[2] but nevertheless, as Peter Brooks states in his essay on the two texts, the Wolf-Man wrote his memoir under both the analytic and textual influence of Freud's version of it.[3] As a premier patient of psychoanalysis, and the subject of one of its most famous case histories, the Wolf-Man's own story is predicated on what he already knew to have been written about him. It is striking that at no point does the Wolf-Man contradict or quarrel with the Freudian text. He does, however, add information about his childhood that is absent from Freud's version.

One such tidbit is that at age five the Wolf-Man's governess read *Don Quijote* in a French children's version to him and his sister. He says that "This book made a tremendous impression on me, but gave me more pain than joy, as I could not accept the idea that this Don Quijote, so dear to my heart, was a fool" (16). *Don Quijote* is not the first book that he knew, however. Sometime before age five, a different governess read Russian translations of Grimm's fairy tales to the children, and supplemented them with excerpts from *Uncle Tom's Cabin*, which terrified the boy. But beyond remarking that the fairy tales were enjoyable and Stowe's novel upsetting, the Wolf-Man forms no literary judgments of those two works. His only slightly later reception of the *Quijote*, though, provides the first clue to a psychoanalytic understanding of his later "Hispanism." He loved Don Quijote, but could not bear the idea that he was a fool. He says that "I felt I could only reconcile myself to this if Don Quijote, at least before his death, recognized his folly. When I was assured of this and shown the picture, on the last page of the book, of a Catholic priest receiving a confession from Don Quijote, I was pacified, for I told myself a priest could not receive confession from a fool" (16). *Don Quijote* provides the Wolf-Man with a way of escaping from his own folly, because he believes that in the act of confession, a fool ceases to be a fool. If a priest can be found to hear a man's confession, that man, of necessity, cannot be entirely mad. The act of confessing to someone *itself* erases folly. Thus the pictures in a children's version of *Don Quijote* provide the Wolf-Man with a way out of narrative isolation. Because he found someone to hear his confession— in this case Freud, a kind of confessor, but not entirely a priest—he is absolved of his own madness. Brooks says that

> The presence of the analyst as narrator and potential narrator "dialogizes" the discourse of the analysand. [...] In this medium of in-between—Freud, we remember, called the transference a Zwischenreich—the "true" narrative lies in-between, in the process of exchange; it is the product of two discourses playing against one another, often warring with one another, working towards recognitions mutually acknowledged but internalized in different ways.[4]

Students of the novel will find that this dialogic structure, theorized first by Bakhtin, is a clear description of the process of the narrative of *Don Quijote*, which occurs by means of the two-volume-long dialogue between Sancho and the Knight. The Wolf-Man's childhood reception of and problems with interpreting *Don Quijote* provide him with a model that informs his own position in the psychoanalytic situation; the Wolf-Man's narrative is structured, at least in part, specifically by his reading of *Don Quijote*.

A further allusion to *Don Quijote* appears a little later, when the Wolf-Man recalls Mr. W., an elderly French gentleman who was a family friend. His looks "always reminded [the Wolf-Man] of Cervantes' Knight of the Mournful Countenance. This, however, was only in appearance. In reality W. had a cheerful disposition and really enjoyed life" (29). Mr. W. only *looks* (to the Wolf-Man) like Don Quijote—that is, looks Spanish—but his appearance does not reveal the truth of his personality or of his nationality. The mention of Mr. W. is significant in that it is the first instance of the Wolf-Man attaching a Spanish or "Hispanized" identity to someone in order to gratify his own desire, even when there are no grounds for the attribution of that identity. The process of "Hispanizing" an object of desire that begins here with Mr. W. acquires much more elaborate and disturbing effects in the Wolf-Man's relationship with Therese, the woman who later becomes his wife.

The pivotal chapter of the Wolf-Man's story is titled "Castles in Spain" and deals with his stay in a Bavarian sanatorium, the failure of his treatment there, which ultimately led him to Freud, and the beginning of his love affair with Therese. The Wolf-Man's first impressions of her are of "an extraordinarily beautiful woman," older than himself, dressed as a Turkish woman for a ball to be held at the sanatorium. "As she was definitely a southern type, with somewhat oriental characteristics, this costume suited her very well [...]" (49). He becomes obsessed with her "exotic" appearance, and finally discovers, by way of a fellow patient, a "Russian lady from Odessa," that the woman to whom he is so attracted is Sister Therese, a nurse. According to the woman from Odessa, Therese's father and mother—the latter supposedly of Spanish birth—were dead, and Therese herself is divorced from a doctor by whom she has had one daughter (this mention is the daughter's only appearance in the text). The Wolf-Man then mentions that "[t]he information that Therese's mother was Spanish interested me particularly since it gave me a clue to her noticeably Mediterranean features" (50). What I found most striking about this comment is its concern with determining the ethnic origins of the beloved on the basis of her appearance. Therese "looks" Mediterranean and Oriental and Southern to the Wolf-Man, but he wants her origin to be more clearly specified, and is entranced when he discovers a particularly *Spanish* heritage. Her looks are, for the Wolf-Man, a key to where she comes from, and his desire for her is fed by that knowledge. According to the Wolf-Man's story, Therese told him about her Spanish origin in their first private meeting:

> It was a very romantic story. Her father was German. Her maternal grandmother, a Spanish woman, was married the first time to a Spanish officer who was said to have been killed in a duel. This grandmother was a singer, widely travelled, and was married three times. As her third husband was German, the daughter from her first marriage went to Germany also, and later met and married Therese's father. (54)

It is after he learns from Therese of her Spanish background that the Wolf-Man says "Thus I suddenly began to be infatuated with Spain, for which I had formerly felt no particular interest. During my psychoanalysis Professor Freud dwelt extensively on this Hispanism, because in his opinion it was to be understood in psychoanalytic terms" (55). It turns out that the Wolf-Man had an aunt, a Polish opera singer, who regaled him and his sister with stories of her travels in Spain. The children then heard this same aunt sing the role of Rosina in Rossini's *Barber of Seville* in St. Petersburg. Freud suggested to the Wolf-Man that because this aunt shared his mother's first name, Alexandra, the Wolf-Man had refracted his incestuous love for his mother through her, knowing all the while that "[a]lthough she was actually Polish by birth, I saw in her a Spanish woman, the more so because she impersonated one on the stage in the part of Rosina. Thus behind my Hispanism the Oedipus complex was hiding, the unconscious desire to possess the mother" (56). What most interests me here is the fallacy of the Wolf-Man's self-described "Hispanism." In his aunt he loves something that is only in the most tangential way an appearance or phantom of Spanishness. As in the case of Mr. W., the allusion to Spanish characteristics is a way of saying who or what a person is *not* rather than of knowing who they are. Mr. W. looks—to the Wolf-Man—like Don Quijote, but the appearance is false to who he really is; further, the opera-singing aunt is not a real Spanish woman, she only plays one on the stage. The Wolf-Man's statement "I saw in her a Spanish woman" indicates that "Spanish" is an idea he creates and projects onto a woman who is somehow prohibited or otherwise problematic for him. To invoke an idea of Spain in this way is to confuse the family lineages and social structures that interrupt or threaten his desire. Therese's "Spanishness" is similarly vexed.

Both the Wolf-Man and Therese vacillated before confirming their love for each other. The Wolf-Man left the Bavarian sanatorium where he had met her and wandered from doctor to doctor until he found Freud in January, 1910. Freud encouraged him to reunite with Therese, but only after several months of analysis. Before their reunion, the Wolf-Man decided to travel to Spain with a physician named Dr. D., who had referred him to Freud. The trip was scheduled to coincide with the two and a half months that Freud would be on his summer vacation. Dr. D., who liked to gamble, insisted on stops in Geneva and Biarritz before going on to the Wolf-Man's preferred Iberian destinations: Lisbon and Madrid, and then Granada and Seville. After the cool weather at the casino at Biarritz the travelers found Lisbon hot and uncomfortable, and according to the Wolf-Man, as soon as they arrived in Madrid Dr. D. tried to change their plans and return to Vienna. The Wolf-Man's response to this is to psychoanalyze Dr. D.:

> Dr. D. was of the Greek Orthodox faith, as his father had been baptized, but his Jewish ancestors had come from Spain, and therefore it *seemed* to me *reasonable* to *suppose* that the uneasiness which he felt in this country had roots somewhere in his unconscious and was connected with the persecution of the Jews during the Inquisition. (85; emphasis added)

Nowhere does the text mention what *Dr. D.* may have said were his own reasons for wanting to leave Spain; all it gives is the Wolf-Man's *supposition* that a history of anti-Semitism made Spain uncomfortable for Dr. D. But these suppositions are projections. All they confirm is that the *Wolf-Man* associates Spain with anti-Semitism, and knows that once there were Spanish Jews—that is, that there can be an association between the identities Jewish and Spanish.

The men ended up returning to Vienna without visiting Andalucia, and soon after that Freud met and approved of Therese. The Wolf-Man and Therese planned to marry as soon as he finished his analysis. But the First World War intervened. Therese came to visit the Wolf-Man and his family in Russia, but anti-German feeling was running high in the family and in town. The fact that Therese spoke neither Russian nor French did not help matters. Still, the Wolf-Man notes, "her definitely southern looks were her only advantage, for anybody might have taken her for Italian or Spanish but never German" (96). Despite political and family conflict eventually the couple did marry, but then they were forced into exile because of the Russian Revolution. Nevertheless, from 1919, when he did another short analysis with Freud, Therese and the Wolf-Man lived peacefully in Vienna. He worked in an insurance company, and those years seem to have been uneventful. Until 1938, that is, for almost twenty years, their "life ran its normal course, without any extraordinary events" (115). But in March of 1938 Hitler annexed Austria. The Wolf-Man says that Therese "took a pessimistic view of the results of the Anschluss," but also that he "even had the impression that Therese, who was *of course* of *German birth*, was proud of her fellow countrymen" (118–19; emphasis added). Yet he notes that Therese's mood declined remarkably in this period. He then adds that the rise of anti-Semitic rioting and other kinds of persecution caused a wave of suicides among the Jews of Vienna. Peter Gay corroborates this in his biography of Freud. At one point "Anna Freud asked her father, 'Wouldn't it be better if we all killed ourselves?' Freud's response was characteristic: 'Why? Because they would like us to?'"[5] Therese remarked to the Wolf-Man that she found the actions of the Jews who had committed suicide courageous. A few days later when he came home from work, she said to him:

"Do you know what we're going to do?"
"Well, what?"
"We'll turn on the gas."

The Wolf-Man responded: "What gives you such a crazy idea? We aren't Jews" (119). He set her remark aside. A week later he told Therese that he and other employees at the insurance company were now going to be required to produce proof that they were of Aryan descent. He was a little worried because the only documentation he had was his League of Nations passport, but he said to Therese that at least it would be no trouble to get *her* documents from her hometown of Wurzburg. When he mentioned this city,

Therese gave me such a strange look that I asked her what was the matter and why she looked at me in such a peculiar way. "It's nothing…" she answered, and looked quite normal again." (120)

A few days later, one of the many swastika flags that had been hung from buildings in Vienna in celebration of the Anschluss appeared outside their bedroom window. All that night a howling wind slammed the flag against the glass, awakening them again and again. The next day when he returned home from work, the Wolf-Man found messages of warning at the apartment door: "'Don't turn on the light—danger of gas.' Therese was sitting near the gas jet, bent over the kitchen table" (121). She had been dead for hours.

The Wolf-Man insistently searches for "the real cause of Therese's terrible decision, and whether and in what way Hitler's invasion of Austria might have triggered it," but he comes to no conclusions (123). The memoir ends with an epilogue though, in which the Wolf-Man discusses a visit to Therese's brother in Munich in 1939. This brother, Josef, "was seven years older than Therese, and the relationship between the brother and the sister had been rather a cool one, as they were of completely different characters" (129). Because the Wolf-Man "found everything that Therese had told [him] of her Spanish ancestry interesting and somehow mysterious," he mentioned it to her brother. The brother's response was "Spanish? That's news to me. [...] But our grandmother is said to have had an affair with an officer of Bavarian nobility" (129). The Wolf-Man cannot understand this information, or why Therese would falsify her history. Referring to the episode of her reaction to his mention of her records in Wurzburg, the Wolf-Man makes the convoluted statement that

> in the Hitler period it would have been even better to have a German grandmother than a Spanish one, and anyhow Therese could have said that the authorities in Wurzburg had made a mistake in the information they gave out. (130)

The question of Therese's origins tormented the Wolf-Man long after her death. In 1947 he wrote to Wurzburg to get her documents (he needed them to apply for Austrian citizenship), but was informed that they had been burned when the building containing them was bombed in the war. This event and her brother's comments place Therese's Spanishness utterly in doubt, and the Wolf-Man is left with several questions that gnaw at him until the very end of the memoir: Did Therese invent her Spanish lineage? Why? Why did she kill herself? What did the Anschluss have to do with it? Therese's identity remains in doubt, but the Wolf-Man's desire to determine it is certain. We cannot know why she killed herself, but the Wolf-Man's narrative places her suicide squarely in the context of the Anschluss, rising anti-Semitism, and the menace of background checks and racist laws. The Spanishness he attributes to her thus begins to slide into a connotative realm parallel to or superimposed upon Jewishness. One of the most important texts about the Wolf-Man's case does not discuss his Hispanism, but nevertheless illuminates the way that this slippage or transposition of meaning works. According to Nicholas Abraham and Maria Torok, the

Wolf-Man expresses prohibited words very indirectly, by using synonyms for the lateral meanings of the prohibited words, instead of the words themselves; the word actually appearing in his text they then call a "cryptonym," a code word which can nevertheless be lexically traced to the word it is meant to hide.[6] The process is complicated by the fact that the Wolf-Man is multilingual—it takes place across Russian, English, German, and French. Torok and Abraham, do not, to my knowledge, extend the metaphor of the cryptonym to the level of national or ethnic meaning, but it is evident that a similar process is at work in the Wolf-Man's fantastic reconstitution of Therese as Spanish. Given the historical and narrative context, easy to read "Spanish" as a cryptonym for "Jewish." I think it is possible to take the reading further, too, and to read (in the Wolf-Man's story, at least) "Jewish" as a code word for some kind of unbearable and unintelligible femininity. From the first time he laid eyes on her, the Wolf-Man was absorbed with a desire to fix and define what he saw as Therese's "mysterious" ethnicity. His desire is characterized by an urgency to find out and label her difference from him. The idea of a phantom Spain covers an anxiety over ethnicity: one's own, as well as that of the Other. The anxiety comes from an inability to pin down the language, race, or nationality of the other, to name it, legislate it, appropriate, or fictionalize it. Therese's dubious Spanishness is, for the Wolf-Man, itself a "Castle in Spain," a "chateau en Espagne," a castle in the air: a projection that hopes to fill a chasm of doubt with an illusion of walled and turreted, unassailable solidity. It is odd that nowhere does the Wolf-Man ask himself if Therese might be Jewish—that idea never occurs to him, and yet all the while he remains obsessed by the question of her Spanishness. The Wolf-Man's enthusiasm for Therese's looks conflates "Oriental," "Turkish," "Southern," "Mediterranean," and "Spanish" in a way typical of the Orientalism of the Romantics. But his Romanticism comes into harsh conflict with the very unromantic historical realities of the Nazi period. The romantic idea of Spain is founded on Orientalism. The knowledge that the Iberian peninsula was settled and civilized for 800 years by Muslims, and had a thriving Jewish population (until after 1492) when first Jews and later Muslims were given orders to convert to Catholicism or leave, makes Spain conveniently Oriental and exotic to a romantic European imagination. It becomes a kind of nearer Near East: but that proximity is the problem. Because the romantic successfully avoids the fact that Spain is European and Christian and Jewish and Muslim and North African—that is, represses its paradoxical similarities and differences from him—Spain can remain sublime. The function of Spain in *modernism*, though, is that it marks the failure of Romanticism by way of a conflicted awareness of difference, an *inability* fully to repress the awareness that the Other and I have more in common than I would like to admit, and what is more, that my fantasies or my power are unable to define and limit the Other's difference. For the

Wolf-Man, Spain is both foreign and familiar, romantic and modern, the point where the wish to define the ethnicity, boundaries, and origins of the Other collapses into itself.

Brooks's essay discusses the undecidability of the case of the Wolf-Man, which he says

> becomes a particularly acute issue in the question of origins. The specification of origins should be of the utmost importance in any etiological explanation: to understand causes, one must get back to the beginning. [...] We know what we are because we can say where we are, and we know this because we can say where we came from.[7]

Brooks is writing about the question of origins and etiology in psychoanalytic narrative, but I think that his observations have a further political meaning relevant to the Wolf-Man and Therese's story. In terms of racism, the determination of origins is a matter of life and death. No undecidability is allowed. In the Wolf-Man's and Therese's experience of history under the Nazis, the question of origins is of crucial importance. In such a situation, one knows who one is not only because one knows where one comes from, but also because one knows where other people come from. One's own location and survival are determined by narrating not what one is, but what one is *not*. This self-identification by way of negation is evident in what the Wolf-Man says when Therese suggested a double suicide: "What gives you such a crazy idea? We aren't Jews" (119).

Similarly, the Wolf-Man uses Spain as a way of articulating an anxiety about what he is not, what Therese somewhere is, and then again, what she may not be. The idea of Spain is the emblem of a desire for an unattainable yet indispensable certainty about ethnic origins, national boundaries, religion, and identity. The Wolf-Man's narrative sacrifices Therese, an undecidable but still clearly feminine Other, to this desire. The Wolf-Man's desire to know about and revel in Therese's "exotic" Spanish origins is a desire for ignorance—of whom she might articulate *herself* to be. It also emphasizes the degree to which the question of ethnicity is an obsessive one. By the end of his story, it is evident that the Wolf-Man can hardly tolerate the gap in his naming of Therese's origins—origins that were only pleasurable when they were products of his own fantasy. Slavoj Žižek's *The Sublime Object of Ideology* discusses how a totalitarian ideology poses the question "What do you want?" and then itself answers the question for the intolerable "you" as a way of accounting for its own failures. "Fantasy is the answer to this 'Che vuoi?'; it is an attempt to fill out the gap of the question with an answer."[8] The inability to know and to control or identify the desire of the Other is intolerable to the Wolf-Man (as it is to many people and systems). His fantasy of an understanding of the Other (fixing her within geographical, cultural, historic, national boundaries) consoles him moment by moment, but ultimately fails. Similarly, Žižek says that "fantasy is the means for an ideology to take its own failure into account in advance."[9] The fetishized Other is given the role of carrying or embodying the pre-existing knowledge of the inability of a society (or a person) to achieve a "full identity as a closed, homogeneous totality."[10] The totalitarian state demands a perfectly clear enunciation of absolutely certain and fixed national, racial, ethnic, religious, and gendered identities. A totalizing mind may have similar tendencies. It punishes others for infractions that represent its awareness of its own uncertainty, inevitable permeability, maybe of its own need for an Other. Of course this whole structure is predicated on never acknowledging the unknowable difference of the Other's desires. I found myself drawn into that kind of fantasizing, too, and wondering if there might any further biographical information on Therese in other sources. A colleague with whom I discussed this essay asked, "What about her brother in Munich? What happened to him? That might be a clue about Therese." I wondered about her daughter. In the course of our conversation I realized that the key issue for me was not where Therese came from, but why I cared so much; why did I, too, feel the need to locate and fix an idea of who she was? I couldn't stand not knowing, either, because not knowing where she was made me feel lost, too—in reference to the Other. I could not be sure about her either, because the official documents were burned, and there is no trace of the brother, the male who might set the family record straight. The daughter has vanished, and the chance for any kind of dialogue with Therese herself is long gone. The Wolf-Man's questionable Hispanism shows where constructions of the Other fail; it marks a place where history disrupts fantasy. The one thing Don Quijote can never take into account is a wife.

Notes

1 Muriel Gardiner, ed., *The Wolf-Man*, by the Wolf-Man, with *The Case of the Wolf-Man*, by Sigmund Freud and *A Supplement* by Anna Freud. (New York: Hill and Wang [The Noonday Press], 1991 [Basic Books, 1971]). All internal citations refer to this edition.

2 Sigmund Freud, "From the History of an Infantile Neurosis" [1918], *The Standard Edition of the Complete Works of Sigmund Freud*, vol. 17, ed. James Strachey (London: Hogarth Press, 1953), 7–122.

3 Peter Brooks, "Fictions of the Wolf-Man: Freud and Narrative Understanding," *Reading for the Plot: Design and Intention in Narrative* (Cambridge, MA: Harvard University Press,1994 [1982]), 264.

4 Ibid., 283.

5 Peter Gay, *Freud: A Life for Our Time* (New York: Norton, 1988), 622.

6 Nicholas Abraham and Maria Torok, *The Wolf-Man's Magic Word: A Cryptonomy*, trans. Nicholas Rand (Minneapolis, MN: University of Minnesota Press, 1986), 18–19.

7 Brooks, "Fictions of the Wolf-Man," 275–76.

8 Slavoj Žižek, *The Sublime Object of Ideology* (London: Verso, 1989), 114.

9 Ibid., 126.

10 Ibid., 127.

CHAPTER EIGHT

Freud's Spain

Freud's essay "A Disturbance of Memory on the Acropolis" was dedicated to the French novelist Romain Rolland on the occasion of his seventieth birthday, which occurred on January 26, 1936. Because of political disruptions, it took Freud a long time to get the essay published; it finally appeared over a year later, in *Almanach*, 1937. James Strachey mentions in his editor's note to the piece that

> It has been impossible to trace any earlier publication of the paper in German other than that in the Almanach noted above. It should be born in mind that any publications connected with Romain Rolland, as with many other authors, including Thomas Mann and of course all Jewish writers, were suppressed during this period by the Nazis.[1]

The Nazi threat finally caused Freud to leave Vienna for London in June 1938, but until then he carried on working heroically despite the aggravation of his cancer and the ever-increasing political dangers that limited his movements. On March 15 Gestapo soldiers searched Freud's apartment and offices. Anna Freud was arrested by them a week later, then interrogated and released. After international efforts to arrange for visas and other necessary transit documents, Freud, his wife, and Anna finally left Vienna on June 4. Peter Gay notes that Freud made a slip in recording the date in his journal, writing June 3 instead of the 4th. Both Gay and Ernest Jones write about how Freud resisted the idea of "deserting his post" in Vienna. The military metaphor's significance will be apparent later. Jones finally convinced him that, like the second officer of the *Titanic*, he was not leaving his ship, his ship was leaving him.[2] In his first letter from London he had written "the triumphant feeling of liberation is mingled too strongly with mourning, for one had still very much loved the prison from which one has been released."[3] Freud had never been fond of Vienna and yet he felt a sense of loss. He had been forced into exile, had lost a kind of home, the place where psychoanalysis began.

The essay for Rolland predates Freud's move to London by about two years, but it addresses questions of loss and exile that were provoked by Freud's illness and the worsening political situation in Central Europe; it was written at a time when Nazi censorship was already affecting publishing. Gay observes that much of Freud's writing from this period has a valedictory tone, a little bit of "the last sigh" about it. In this piece, in the first paragraph in which he extends his birthday greeting to Rolland, who, having turned seventy was not an extremely young man either, Freud says, "I am ten years older than you, and my powers of production are at an end. All that I can find to offer you is the gift of an impoverished creature, who has seen better days" (239). This gift is the record of an analysis of a memory of a sensation that had been troubling Freud for the "last few years." Freud recalls a trip to the Mediterranean in 1904 with his brother, and their plan, because of a shortage of time, to travel briefly from Trieste to Corfu, and then to return straight home. A business associate of Freud's brother suggested that, instead of going to Corfu, which is unbearably hot in early September, the two should make a quick trip to Athens, where neither of them had ever been before. It had been a lifelong desire of Freud's to travel in Greece, and especially to see the Acropolis. Nevertheless Freud recalls that he and his brother reacted to the friend's suggestion with indecision and great depression, and wandered around Trieste during the siesta not doing much of anything. Finally, when the offices reopened after the mid-day break, they booked their trips to Athens without further ado, despite the fact that just before they had been in "a gloomy state and foreseen nothing but obstacles and difficulties" (240).

A few days later, Freud finally stood on the longed-for surface. The first thought that came to mind was "so all this really does exist, just as we learnt at school!" (241). Freud found this thought surprising, because it showed that "the person who gave expression to the remark was divided, far more sharply than was usually noticeable, from another person who took cognizance of the remark; and both were astonished, though not by the same thing" (241). The first was astonished because he had to believe in something he had not formerly believed in—the Acropolis; the second was stunned because he had been "unaware that the real existence of Athens, the Acropolis, and the landscape around it had ever been objects of doubt" (241). Freud tries to analyze the situation by making a connection between his affect at Trieste and his sensation of astonishment on the Acropolis, because both moments contained elements of disbelief. In Trieste, the sadness came from a feeling that it would be too difficult to get to the desired destination, and the trip "would have been so lovely" (242). Freud says that the chance to go to Athens "is one of those cases of too good to be true [in English in original] that we come across so often" (242), an example of the incredulity that arises in some people when they feel that they have been granted a favor of which they are not worthy. Their good fortune disrupts the expectation of a punishing fate that "is a materialization [...] of the severe superego within us..." (243). Freud says that he is not surprised at the force of his reaction on the Acropolis because of "the passionate desire to travel and see the world by which [he] was dominated at school and later" (243). Because his wish was so strong, so was his guilt. This guilt (which I will discuss in a few moments) produced the "momentary feeling: what I see here is not real," a moment of "derealization" (*Entfremdungsgefuhl*) (244).

Derealization is similar to depersonalization. In the first case, the subject feels that a piece of reality is strange to him; in the second it is a piece of himself. Derealization and depersonalization are also related to *déjà vu*, *déjà raconté*, and *fausse reconnaissance*; in the first set of phenomena, the subject rejects objects that are part of its experience; in the second set it appropriates or acknowledges things that it wishes were part of it. One pushes things away, another tries to pull them in. Depersonalization and derealization are ego defense mechanisms, but do not have as thorough an effect as repression. As an example of "a marginal case of this kind of defense," Freud cites the medieval Spanish *romance* "Ay de mi, Alhama," in which the king of Granada, who feels that the loss of Alhama means the end of his hegemony, "will not let it be true[:] he determines to treat the news as 'non arrivé'; burning the letters and killing the messenger who brought them" (246). (I will return to this text in a moment.) Derealization is like doing what the king did: it is a tantrum of denial that everyone (including its perpetrator) knows will change nothing. In Freud's case, the moment of disbelief on the Acropolis was the result of "a sense of guilt [...] attached to the satisfaction in having gone such a long way" from home and from his father, who had had neither the funds nor the education to achieve or appreciate a trip to Athens. Some part of Freud could not believe that he had exceeded "the limitations and poverty of [the] conditions of life in [his] youth" (247). The conflict came because "the essence of success was to have got further than one's father even though to excel one's father was still something forbidden" (247). The moment of disavowal marks the collision of the two currents. It is interesting, too, that Freud writes this essay to Rolland, who is the same age as the brother with whom he traveled to the Acropolis, when Freud himself is very old and sick and near death—that is, in the position of his own father. It is only safe to face the fact that one has gone too far when one is too far gone to go anywhere anymore. Freud concludes the essay with a sad expression: "and now you will no longer wonder that the recollection of this incident on the Acropolis should have troubled me so often since I myself have grown old and stand in need of forbearance and can travel no more" (248). These beautiful and heart-breaking lines evoke a crumbled strength and the nobility of the wreck that recalls it. In them Freud seems identified with the ruins of the Acropolis itself.

The Alhambra is an Acropolis—etymologically and geographically a "high city," too. Freud says that the king "derealizes" the news of the loss of the town of Alhama (20 miles from Granada) because it signifies the end of his dominion: and the most precious jewel in the crown was the palace of the Alhambra. Freud's interest in and knowledge of classical and ancient civilizations is well documented, so it is significant that in this essay about the Acropolis he chooses to illustrate a crucial psychic function with a text from outside the classical canon. Why does he choose a Spanish text, and one so far removed, both historically and geographically, from Greece at the other end of the Mediterranean? Let us remember that Freud's analysis of his sensation on the Acropolis is rooted in a feeling of "filial piety"—a regret that he had gone too far from, and further than, his father. Just before he quotes the second stanza of the poem, Freud sets it up for Rolland like this: "You remember the famous lament of the Spanish Moors 'Ay de mi, Alhama,' which tells how King Boabdil received the news of the fall of his city of Alhama" (246). Now, Alhama was taken by the Marqués of Cádiz on February 28, 1482, when Boabdil's father Muley Hacén, an aged but effective man, was still king of Granada. It was not until July 1482, when Boabdil and his half-brother Youssef took control of Granada, that his father passed momentarily out of the picture.[4] Freud thus made an historical slip that his editor and translator, the otherwise relentlessly correct and correcting James Strachey, missed too. Freud's mistake puts the son where the father should be. It was Boabdil who lost the *Alhambra* in 1492; it was his father Muley Hacén who lost *Alhama* in 1482. The similarity between the two words facilitates their confusion. It is also a first indication of why Freud may have chosen this *romance* rather than a classical text; the *romance*, like Freud's essay, alludes to the story of a son whose filial piety is lacking, and whose chastisement is fulfilled in later years when the son, like his father, must give up his territory to someone else, and go into exile.

The *romance* also makes possible further confusions of identity that are based on Freud's insertion of the son in the father's place. First, Freud identifies with Boabdil; just as Freud treats the news of his own arrival on the Acropolis as *non arrivé*, so does Boabdil (in Freud's version) reject the loss of his kingdom by killing the messenger and burning the letters he brought. Next, the *romance*, written in the language of the Christians, and according to most contemporary critical opinion composed by them, tells of the loss of Alhama to the Christians, but in the voice of the Moors. A Moorish poetic voice tells how the Moors lost the town to the Christians. The effect of this confusion is both to occlude and to emphasize the relationship between Freud and Boabdil. Both here and in the case of the Wolf-Man in the previous chapter, we can see how Spain functions, because of the specificity of its history of *convivencia* and then intolerance of difference, enacted precisely as a result of the conquest of Granada, as a rhetorical symptom of anxiety about location and ethnicity. In this case, Freud, a Jew living in an ever-more anti-Semitic Austria, identifies with a Moor, a Muslim, who lost his kingdom to the Christians. There is no mention of Jews or anti-Semitism in the essay for Rolland, despite the fact that anti-Semitism was an issue that Freud actively engaged in other texts written around this time. Perhaps it is a function of the censorship that Strachey alludes to in his editor's note. Or it may be that the absence of mention of the Jews' loss of their place in Spain in 1492 hits too close to home. Freud can identify with Boabdil because not only for the Moors, but also for the Jews, Spain is a lost home, and a producer of exile.

Freud says that the functions of *non arrivé, fausse reconnaisance, déjà raconté,* and *déjà vu* have in common that they draw on memories and impressions from the subject's past. Freud transposes his present feelings of loss in the essay written when he was eighty years old, about an event that occurred when he was only forty-eight, into an even more distant past, the one when Boabdil lost his own precious and beautiful Acropolis high above Granada. Past and present meet in the conflation (made possible by confusing Boabdil with his father) of Acropolis and Alhambra. Both Acropolis and Alhambra, too, refer to the loss of home—that is, of a connection to his father, and to the city, Vienna, where Freud had built his own empire. The association between the son's imperial ambitions and his relationship with his father appears again in the Rolland essay just after Freud cites the *romance*. As an example of how the sons have come a long way from their childhood life with father, Freud says: "so too, if I may compare such a small event with a greater one, Napoleon, during his coronation as emperor in Notre Dame, turned to one of his brothers—it must no doubt have been the eldest one, Joseph—and remarked, 'What would Monsieur nôtre père have said to this, if he could have been here today?'" (247). Strachey points out in a footnote that this anecdote is usually told of Napoleon's assumption of the iron crown of Lombardy in Milan—a slightly lesser prize than his coronation as Emperor. But the point is to show how the ambition to travel is psychically connected to imperial ambitions, and how both are connected to a desire both to exceed and to stay close to the father. The Alhama example, and to a lesser extent the Napoleon one, show how ambivalent these satisfactions tend to be. Just before the Napoleon anecdote, Freud mentions how traveling can make "one feel [...] like a hero who has performed feats of improbable greatness" (247). Yet in the sentence just before that he states that "a great part of the pleasure of travel [...] is rooted [...] in disatisfaction with home and family" (247). Traveling and empire building have in common their ambivalent relationship with home.

Page du Bois's essay "A Disturbance of Syntax at the Gates of Rome" says that "on the Acropolis, the site of ancient goddess worship, Freud has eyes only for the father."[5] It is true that Freud mentions his mother only once in the essay, and that for him the ambivalence about traveling comes from leaving the father but not necessarily home behind. But it is important to remember that Freud puts his experience on the Acropolis in the same category as moments of *déjà vu* and

fausse reconnaissance, and that those experiences are part of the general structures of the uncanny. The lesson of the uncanny is that the least familiar place
is the most home-like place of all: uncanny sensations refer back to a memory of
the mother's genitals, the place we came from. In this context, Barbara Johnson
mentions in an essay on Toni Morrison's *Sula* that "home is where the phallus
is not."[6] The fear and knowledge of castration that create uncanny sensations
support her observation. But, if we may supplement the visual element, we can
remember that even if "home is where the phallus is not," home is also where
the phallus has been. Freud went as far away from his father-home as he could.
But what did he find so far away, on the Acropolis, so impossibly different in
time, space, and context from his childhood in Vienna? An insistent memory,
one that followed him for thirty-two years, of his father. At the age of eighty, still
thinking of how far he has gone in life, he still cannot think about the Acropolis
without thinking of his father. The most foreign place is where family ties are
most insistently felt.

To have mentioned his mother in the Acropolis essay would have made the
connection between home and the foreign too evident. The father is for Freud a
trace of home; the mother is home itself. If mother surfaces at all in this essay, it
is in connection with Boabdil, weeping and then chided by his mother for losing
their home. He was not, as the other *romance* says, man enough to hold onto
Granada. The implication is that his father was. And because of their conflict,
son and father lose home and empire to each other, and then to an external,
"different" other. None of these conquerors wants to leave home, no matter how
problematic it may be, until he is good and ready. Not Boabdil, not Napoleon,
not Freud; none was ever ready for exile.

And having to leave Vienna for London because of the Nazis was not Freud's
first exile. When he was a little boy, his father, in order to improve the family
fortunes, decided that they would move from Freud's birthplace, the town of
Freiberg in Moravia. They went first to Leipzig, and soon after to Vienna. So
Freud's father was a traveler too, and his traveling made Freud leave home. Peter
Gay quotes him as saying in 1899: "I never felt really comfortable in the city. I
now think that I have never got over the longing for the beautiful woods of my
home, in which (as a memory remaining from those days attests), scarcely able
to walk, I used to run off from my father."[7] In 1931 (or five years before the
Acropolis essay) he wrote, "Deep within me, covered over, there still lives that
happy child from Freiberg, the first-born son of a youthful mother, who had
received the first indelible impression from this air, this soil."[8] This is the way
that Freud writes about his first lost home.

A minor consolation for Freud must have been the frequent visits to Freiberg
he made with various family members during his youth and adolescence. On
one of these trips, probably in 1869 (when Freud was 13) he may have met a child

named Eduard Silberstein. In any case, by 1870, the two boys were fast friends, and in 1871 (at age 15) they made a joint trip back to Freiberg. Silberstein's family shared many social contacts in Freiberg with the Freuds, and the two boys developed crushes on various girls there. They needed a secret language that they could use to discuss these romantic and other private concerns, and they decided to use—the Spanish of the Golden Age. They founded what they called an "Academia Castellana," and by 1871 had started "the joint study of Spanish [...], without teacher, grammar, or dictionary, and based in the reading of a primer [that Walter Boehlich, editor of Freud's letters to Silberstein] has been unable to trace". [9] The primer, judging from references in the letters, "appears to have contained texts by Cervantes and Cecilia Böhl de Faber, including an extract containing the conversation of two dogs, Cipión and Berganza" (xv).

As is well known, Freud took the name Cipión, and Silberstein Berganza,[10] but it is to be suspected because of omissions and errors regarding the *Coloquio de los perros* that Freud never read all of that Exemplary Novel. The editors of these letters, the sum of Freud's writings in Spanish, refer to the clumsiness of their grammar and expression. That clumsiness, though, is crucial to their meaning. Here is a quotation from a letter of March 7, 1875:

[...] *Parte oficial.* Cosas de la Academia Española o Castellana.
Otro punto es, que propone D. Cipión la introducción de siguientos términos en el estilo oficial de la A. E., cuales términos no son nuevos, pero viejos y bien conocidos y merecen ser sacados en limpio para el uso de los miembros de la A.E. Llámanse los miemb. d.l.A.E. "perros", que es su mayor título, que tienen ni tendrán, llamese "Sevilla" el mundo, en que están y el hospital de Sevilla el país en que viven, es decir la Alemania. Llámese en fin el paradero [parador?] , en que están, la cerra [here it is thought that he wanted to say "el cerro"] o si otra palabra es, que quiere decir "Dicke" ["thickness"] y que el famoso Cervantes en el lugar, que V. conoce, ha usado, sea esa otra palabra). Así los m.d.l. A.E. jamás digan de alguien "ha muerto," sino ha salido de Sevilla, jamas digan, ha dejado la Alemania sino ha quitado el hospital de Sevilla y jamás digan, ha viajado en Alemania, de Viena a Berlin, sino digan, ha mudado de cerra [cerro]. Viena llámese con otro nombre y así también Berlin, pero los nombres no quiero proponer, sino dejo a Vm de proponerlos, que viva mil y docientos anos y sea dos mil años mantenido como desea Su D. Cipión (n. 7, 98–99)

(Official Part. Things of the Spanish or Castilian Academy.
Another point is that Don Cipion proposes the introduction of the following terms in the official style of the S.A., which terms are not new, but old and well known and deserve to be taken up for the use of the members of the Spanish Academy. Members of the Spanish Academy shall be called "dogs," which is the best title they could ever have, the world shall be called "Sevilla," and the country they live in the "hospital of Sevilla," that is to say, Germany. The place they live in shall be called "la cerra" [see below], or if it is another word then let it be whatever means "fat or plump or thick" and that it be the word that the famous Cervantes

uses in another place that you know of. Thus the members of the S.A. shall never say of someone, "he has died," but rather, "he has left Sevilla," never shall they say, he has left Germany, but rather, he has left the hospital of Sevilla, they shall never say, he has traveled in Germany from Vienna to Berlin, but rather "he has changed 'cerra.'" Vienna shall be known by another name and so shall Berlin, but I do not wish to propose the names but to leave it to Your Worship to do so, and may you live one thousand two hundred years and may it be thus for two thousand years as desired by Your own Don Cipion.)

Setting grammatical infelicities aside, the crucial part of this letter is that is substitutes Spanish place names for German and Austrian ones. The boys, the two members of the Academia, are *perros*; the world is *Sevilla*, *el hospital de Sevilla* is Germany. Their lodgings (*paradero* for *parador?*) become *un cerro*, perhaps from a reference to "El Cerro Gordo," which appears in Cervantes's play *El trato de Argel*. In a later letter, Berlin becomes Madrid. In other words, the boys, whose deep friendship took hold in Freiberg, the place from which Freud was first exiled, in their fantasies have turned Germany into Spain, a place where ideas of home and exile again coincide. Spain is safe as a supplement for a real location because it marks not mine, but the Other's (the Moors) lost Empire, the Other's lost paradise, the Other's lost home. This is especially apparent in Freud's citation of "Ay de mi, Alhama," which tells not of the Spanish Jews' loss of their homes in Spain, but rather the loss of the Spanish Muslims. The constellation Acropolis/Alhambra/Alhama/Freiberg, the Moor in the Spanish *romance* lamenting and denying loss on the Acropolis, shows that for Freud, because of its connection with *exile*, Spanish is the language not only of the loss of, but also of reconnection with, home.

The only part of the *romance* that Freud quotes in the Acropolis essay is the second verse:

Cartas le fueron venidas
Que Alhama era ganada.
Las cartas echó en el fuego
Y al mensajero matara.

(Letters were sent to him
That said Alhama had been taken
He threw the letters in the fire
And killed the messenger.)[11]

At the beginning of the essay to Rolland, Freud says that the Acropolis memory was one that had been troubling him "for the last few years" (239). These are precisely the years of Hitler's rise. In 1936 in German Europe, letters thrown into the fire has a powerful resonance: Nazi book burnings had already begun. If Freud identified with the Moorish king in his reading of the *romance*, it may have been out of a wish to burn the letters that announced the burnings, to deny the bad news, or at least to delay its arrival. Anti-Semitism was already amply and clearly a part of the Nazi agenda. The loss of the ability to travel that occasioned the writing of the essay for Rolland presages yet another exile. Here and in the case of the Wolf-Man, where Hispanism is also at issue, we can see how Spain comes to signify for persons in dominant social and political positions an anxiety produced by their inability to fix the ethnic provenance of the Other, because of the ways that the undecidability of the location and identity of that Other disturbs the stability of those dominant people. The Wolf-Man, a once wealthy Russian, also writing about the period 1936–38 in Vienna, states in his memoir, "We aren't Jews."[12] But Freud is a Jew; for him, in early life, even with its history as a producer of exile, Spain is a place and Spanish a language that articulate a reconnection to a lost home—and they do so in their medieval and Golden Age texts and contexts. In later life, a Spanish text reminds him that his own location is threatened, and that exile may come again. As an old man in the shadow of the Nazis, "las cartas echó en el fuego." As a boy, when he could still re-write his life in Cervantine Spanish rather than being written by it, his motto was, for better or worse "No mano otra toque esa carta".[13] The letters in Spanish preserve and document an ambivalent reassurance that what seems most foreign can be full of souvenirs of home. Literature makes time-travel possible: modernity and the Golden Age mutually inform each other.

Notes

1 Sigmund Freud, "A Disturbance of Memory on the Acropolis" [1937], *The Standard Edition of the Complete Works of Sigmund Freud*, vol. 22, ed. and trans. James Strachey (London: The Hogarth Press, 1963), 238. All internal citations refer to this edition.

2 Gay, *Freud: A Life for Our Time*, 625.

3 Ibid., 629.

4 J. H. Elliot, *Imperial Spain, 1469–1716* (New York: St. Martin's Press, 1963), 48.

5 Page du Bois, "A Disturbance of Syntax at the Gates of Rome," *Stanford Literature Review* 2.2 (Fall 1985): 186.

6 Johnson, "'Aesthetic' and 'Rapport' in Toni Morrison's *Sula*," 79.

7 Gay, *Freud: A Life for Our Time*, 9.

8 Ibid.

9 *The Letters of Sigmund Freud to Eduard Silberstein, 1871–1881*, ed. Walter Boehlich, trans. Arnold J. Pomerans (Cambridge, MA; Belknap Press of Harvard University Press, 1970), xv.

10 Stanislav Zimic's "El casamiento engañoso y Coloquio de los perros," *Boletin de la Biblioteca de Menendez Pelayo* 70 (1994): 55–125 is the first publication I am aware of to allude to these writings.

11 "Ay de mi, Alhama," in *Spanish Ballads*, ed. C. Colin Smith (New York: Pergamon, 1964)

12 Wolf-Man, *The Wolf-Man*, ed. Gardiner, 119.

13 Boehlich (ed.), *Letters* 19.

CHAPTER NINE

You'll See Your Castles in Spain Back in Your Own Backyard

The bird with feathers of blue
Is waiting for you
Back in your own backyard
You'll see your castles in Spain
Through your window pane
Back in your own backyard

Oh you can go to the East
Go to the West
But someday you'll come
Weary at heart
Back where you started from
You'll find your happiness lies
Right under your eyes
Back in your own backyard

from "Back in Your Own Backyard" (Al Jolson/Billy Rose/D. Dreyer)

This song functions through apostrophe; not only does it address an absent other, it multiplies and intensifies a prismatic absence, addressing "You" in order to remind you that you are not "there." The song specifies that you are not happy. You are not happy because you are not There—where the bluebird of happiness is. Happiness lies in wait for you; the bluebird is a bird of prey. It is more like Poe's raven than some animated messenger of joy. Or perhaps it has been dismantled, as by a cat, separated as it is in the lyrics from its feathers of blue. In any case, it is waiting for you, back there.

Your backyard is your own. Back there, you return. The strange phrase "Back in Your Own Backyard" announces a return twice ("Back" is there twice) and ownership twice, too: this is your own backyard, not just your backyard. "Own" is an intensifier; you are indissolubly connected to a place you own, but where you are not. The intimate space of the backyard is the space behind the home. Whether behind a tenement building or a suburban cottage, the backyard is specifically not the space of the front yard. It is not public like the front yard, but it is not private, either. It is the place where dirty laundry hangs privately out in public. The backyard is open and hidden at the same time. A backyard is an open secret. The backyard is a conjunction of public and private. The song presents a conjunction of past and future: when you return (sometime in the future) you will be at home in the past. In this future past, you will see "your castles in Spain / through your window pane." You will see Spain in your backyard, which is not in Spain. You will see Spanish castles[1] through your window pane and they will be back in your own non-Spanish backyard. You will be looking out at them from the inside, through a pane of glass: your pane of glass, your own windowpane. Your castles in Spain will be framed by your domestic window frame, and the pane is what will separate you from your castles and also unite you with them by transmitting your gaze. The song pulls at You, pulling You back to the place in back, Your place.

The phrase "castles in Spain" is first attested in the West in *Le Roman de la Rose* (c.1235):

> Et je vais te dire une fière merveille:
> certaines fois il adviendra
> que tu croiras tenir entre tes bras
> la belle au clair visage, toute nue,
> comme si elle était devenue
> à jamais ton amie et ta compagne.
> Alors tu feras des châteaux en Espagne
> et tu auras une vaine joie
> aussi longtemps que tu te laisseras porter
> par cette charmante penseé
> où il n'y a que mensonge et que fable...[2]

It comes into English with Chaucer's translation of the *Romaunt of the Rose* about forty years later (c. 1277):

> (2568) And wite thou wel, withoute were,
> That thee shal [seme] somtyme that nyght
> That thou has hir that is so bright
> Naked bitwene thynne armes there,
> All sothfastnesse as though it were.
> (2573) Thou shalt make castels thane in Spayne,
> And dreme of joye, all but in vayne,
> And thee deleiten of right nought,
> While thou so slomrest in that thought
> That is so swete and delitable,
> The which, in soth, nys but fable [,][3]

After Chaucer the phrase returns to France, appearing in the rondeaux of Charles d'Orleans.[4] Al Jolson releases the first version of "Back in Your Own Backyard," with the phrase "castles in Spain," in 1928.[5] "Castles in Spain" is the phrase of choice for the Wolf-Man when he decides to write about his "Hispanism" and love for his wife Therese, who kills herself in Vienna shortly after the Nazi Anschluss takes effect in March, 1938. Billie Holiday's version of the song is recorded in New York City in January, 1938. This is just before the start of the Second World War in Europe, in the midst of the Great Depression, in a Manhattan that Billie Holiday found more racist than the South. Donald Clarke, one of her biographers, upon comparing her version of the song to Jolson's sentimental one, says, "Lady makes you believe it, as though remembering an idyllic childhood that she should have had, but didn't."[6]

In fact, a yearning for what one has never had in the first place marks all of the canonical uses of the phrase "castles in Spain." In this respect nostalgia is like a screen memory:[7] it expresses the present, even though it narrates itself in terms of the past. The specific fantasy in Guillaume de Lorris is an erotic fantasy: the speaker dreams that he holds the body of his soft, naked female lover in his arms, but he is deceived. He is dreaming, and the French and English texts set his frustrated fantasizing in the following terms: "Thou shalt make castels thanne in Spayne, / And dreme of joye, all but in vayne."[8] Some critics argue that "Spain" here has no particular meaning, and that it is only used for purposes of rhyming, as in Rodgers' and Hart's famous couplet, "The rain in Spain / Falls mainly in the plain."[9] But when Charles d'Orleans was imprisoned by the English after the battle of Agincourt, nostalgia for his estates in France provoked the following verses that narrate his expansionist hopes: "Et fais chasteaulz en Espagne et en France." This too is all fantasy. Dreams of Spanish castles offset the anxiety of not triumphing, not building, not expanding one's domains—of failing and losing, even. There is another Old French use which has "châteaux en Asie"[10] to communicate a distant object of desire. But the phrase from 1235 or so, using Spain, is the one that has endured in the popular culture of empire through the centuries. There is a parallel between building castles in Spain and erotic conquest. This parallel is an example of how empire always narrates itself over a feminized body. Here the connection is explicit: castle in Spain = erotic satisfaction. The *Roman de la Rose* is explicitly about the conquest of the feminine. And yet the failure of the construction is built right into it. In 1235 and 1277, castles in Spain are in danger. They are the real and symbolic locations of conflict between Christians and Muslims. They are fabulous: if they are Moorish, they even have running water. If they are Christian, they are besieged. Desired and anxiety-provoking: a castle in Spain is the fantastic architecture of imperial ambition. In 1479, in the Alcázar of Segovia, Spain ("alcázar" is a Moorish Arabic name for a fortified castle which has passed unchanged into Spanish), Ferdinand and Isabel become the monarchs of a unified Spain. Aragon and Castile (Castilla means the land of castles) are brought together in their marriage, and the child they produce is the Spanish Empire. It is no coincidence that the Alcázar of Segovia should be the model for Sleeping Beauty's castle in the animated Disney film. The allure of the Spanish castle is very durable. Tourist brochures from Segovia emphasize the relationship between that city's medieval alcázar and Disney's Sleeping Beauty castle. On their marriage ten years earlier (that is, in 1469) Ferdinand and Isabel adopted the motto "Ne Plus Ultra" for the modern state that would come out of the unification of their kingdoms. The *ne plus ultra* is that which cannot be exceeded, the best, the extreme, the maximum, the top. The device accompanying the motto shows the Pillars of Hercules as a pair of parallel columns; these are symbols of the two mountainous promontories that shape the Strait of Gibraltar and mark the end of the Mediterranean Sea and the known world. Just beyond the Pillars of Hercules, the flat sea dropped off into the void at the edge of the flat earth. In 1492, with the discovery and the beginning of the conquest of the Americas, Ferdinand and Isabel dropped the "ne," and changed the motto to "plus ultra": there's always MORE! Not coincidentally, this device is the precursor for the dollar sign, $, which should properly be written with two vertical strokes. The two vertical lines are the pillars of Hercules, and the S-shaped line is the banner upon which "ne plus ultra" or "plus ultra" is inscribed. Interestingly, the emblem that became the dollar sign, the mark of global capitalism, simultaneously says "No more!" and "More, more, more!" It succinctly defines commodity fetishism.

When Columbus, in the employ of Ferdinand and Isabel, sailed through the Pillars and out into the Atlantic, he was going to the East and West at the same time. Empire building pays surprisingly little attention to maps and cardinal points, because, after all, it is all in the imperialist's head. You'll be weary at heart someday when you come back where You started from. Origin and return collide, with the result that nobody's home. It is curious in this respect to note that no one is sure where Christopher Columbus's body is buried. It is possible to go to see the tiny coffins of Ferdinand and Isabel, though. The Catholic Monarchs are buried in the heart of what used to be a most wonderful Muslim city in Europe: Granada. Home is where the heart is weary: back where you started from, which (the departure point of fantasy) is always somewhere else. According to this song, empire is a mission of repetition, return, and failed retrieval. You will find—not what you are looking for, but rather that "Your happiness lies." Your happiness does not, cannot tell the truth, because what You want is not back there. Or, perhaps Your happiness lies, dead and buried like a family pet back in Your own backyard.

Clarke errs when he states that Billie Holiday invokes or evokes her childhood here. But he is correct in suggesting that she was singularly well-placed to reveal the historical and psychological nuances of this song. Billie Holiday was not one to deceive or sugarcoat in her singing. She was not subject to the ventriloquism that operated in the careers and styles of some Black singers of her era. Perhaps that is why she was never voted the "number one" singer in the major polls of her day. Sometimes it was Ella Fitzgerald, followed by forgettable names. (Billie Holiday did come in second once or twice.) Of her career she said, "In this business, you smile to keep from throwing up." Smiling and singing prevent regurgitation; the repetition compulsion that "Back in Your Own Backyard" textualizes is worked over, if not worked through, in Holiday's version. Billie Holiday enunciates the double entendres of what others had sung as an innocent ditty of adolescent nostalgia. The texts that establish the phrase, "Castles in Spain" do so as an element of imperial fetishism in which displacement, colonization, and feminization happen at once, even while impossibility and regret attend the conqueror. In this 1938 hit song, gender is absent. The basic challenge to all performers: is the beloved a he or a she?—that is, sexual binarism—is not here. All we have is You.

> You'll see.
> You'll come.
> You'll find.

Of course there are resonances with Julius Caesar's "veni, vidi, vici." Right under Your eyes, happiness lies, and gets away with it. Billie Holiday's version of the song uses a literal rendering of the lyrics to disperse narratives of fantastic dominance, and to induce and acknowledge the panic that always attends empire.

Notes

1 See also Jimi Hendrix's song "Spanish Castle Magic," *Axis: Bold as Love* (Bella Godiva Music, 1967).

2 Guillaume de Lorris, *Le Roman de la Rose*, vol. I (Paris: Librairie Honoré Champion Éditeur, 1983), 95–95, ll. 2423–34.

3 Geoffrey Chaucer, *Romaunt of the Rose*, *Romaunt of the Rose [and] Minor Poems, The Complete Works*, vol. 1, ed. Walter W. Skeat (Oxford: Clarendon Press, 1894), 178, ll. 2568–78.

4 Charles d'Orléans, "Rondeaux 54," *Ballades et rondeaux* (Paris: Librarie générale française, 1992).

5 Al Jolson, Billy Rose and D. Dreyer, "Back in Your Own Backyard" (New York: Columbia Records, January 3, 1928).

6 Donald Clarke, *Wishing on the Moon: The Life and Times of Billie Holiday* (New York: Viking, 1994), 154.

7 Freud, "Screen Memories," 301–22.

8 Chaucer, *Romaunt of the Rose*, 178, ll. 2573–74.

9 *My Fair Lady*, dir. George Cukor (1964).

10 See the 11th *OED Online* entry for "castle": "As to the [French] *faire des châteaux en Espagne* (found in 13th c.) see Littré; since it varied with *châteaux en Asie, en Albanie*, it appears that the phrase at bottom meant only to build castles in a foreign country where one had no standing-ground, Spain finally taken as the nearest Moorish country to Christendom, or perhaps with some reference to the arms of Castile."

CHAPTER TEN

The Route of Writing[1]

El ingenioso hidalgo Don Quijote de la Mancha[2] was written, or "composed" (*compuesto* is the Spanish word) by Miguel de Cervantes Saavedra, and appeared in print in 1605. The title page of the book in which these words appear does not read, "The Life of Don Quijote," or "The Story of Don Quijote," or "The Adventures of Don Quijote." It is just imprinted with a name and identifying adjectival information. It is like a plain tombstone. Or it is like a business card, or more accurately like an old-fashioned social calling card, the kind of thing that lovers in Victorian novels drop into little baskets when they go to visit their beloveds, but do not find them at home. The calling card reads, "I was, and am still, here." There is an identity between the person named and the inscription. Don Quijote and the text itself are inseparable. Person and text cannot be divided. The author, or "composer," permits no distance between the text and the named being; no narrative genre's name impedes the autonomous enunciation, *ex nihilo*, of the presence of *el ingenioso hidalgo* Don Quijote de la Mancha. So when someone picks up what we call today the First Part of *Don Quijote*, that is, the part published in 1605 (the Second Part did not appear until ten years later), that person holds human being in those reading hands. That reader holds a human subjectivity that is made of writing, reading, and printing. And when *El ingenioso hidalgo Don Quijote de la Mancha* is read, the reader's subjectivity passes through a moment that is unrepeatable and irrevocable, the result of which is that Don Quijote and the reader can never be parted. This is true even if all the reader has ever read of Don Quijote is the title page, or even just that first line. Cervantes names neither book nor character in the title; what is printed there is, rather, all of human life.

In order to understand this better, you may wish to consider making an attempt to recall the first time that you ever read your own name. Perhaps the reader has never done this before; nevertheless, there is no text like the present. When did I first read my own name? How old was I? Was I a child or an adult? Where was I? How did I feel? Am I able to remember that moment? Is that moment lost in the haze of infantile amnesia? What about writing for the first time? Perhaps the reader or the reader's ancestors or loved ones conserve a memory or textual evidence of this work. What was the first thing you ever wrote? Think of the tremendous intellectual, psychic, and physical invest-ment required to produce that first legible word. Everything you had to give, in addition to a good deal from your teacher, went into that word. You wrote it, your teacher having composed your faculties sufficiently so that you could bring them into harmony and do it. At that moment there was no separation between you, the writing subject, and that word. A whole life goes into the writing of one person's name. It is cruel to say of a person, "He can't even spell his own name." The implication of the insult is not that the person is illiterate, but rather that he is stupid. It also implies a person who cannot be bothered to get even the most crucial details of his own life right—so what can he do for me? Most people take extreme care in the spelling of their own name. A feeling of outrage will tend to accompany the experience of reading one's own name, misspelled. Is this because of the herculean effort involved in learning to write it that first time? Is it because I am that name, and there can be no disjunction between me and the accurate spelling? I have friends whom I have known for years who persist in adding the letter "e" to my last name. Who is the person to whom they refer? I know who they mean, but their inaccuracy distorts the knowledge I think I have of myself. I am lost in transcription. This almost happens to Don Quijote, too.

The first chapter of the book is a tale of origins that breaks in every way from the expected formula for beginnings. That formula seeks to meet a yearning for certainty that is closely tied to anxieties about paternity and power. The child who asks, "Where did I come from?" has (at least) two problems. One is, "Who is my father?," that is, where do I fit in the system of society beyond my mother's body? Another, implicit in the question, "Where did I come from?," is that the speaking subject who asks that question knows that it did not create itself. And yet the knowledge that I did not create my own body interrupts all kinds of fantasies of control and omnipotence. Teresa de Lauretis has said that much of the work of canonical narrative is to affirm the fantasy of the autochthonous nature of man[3]—the idea that I have given birth to myself, that the mother is incidental or not necessary at all; ultimately, that I do not need anybody, that I am not and never was dependent upon anybody else's body: especially not a female body. So the beginning of *Don Quijote* addresses these anxieties head-on. Instead of supplying information that clearly indicates who, what, when, where, why, and how it all began, it is veiled in uncertainties and unclarified conditions.[4] The very first sentence will not specify the location of the action; it says, "En un lugar de la Mancha, de cuyo nombre no quiero acordarme [...] ("In a village of La Mancha, which I prefer to leave un-named") (I.i). The time is unclear also: "no ha mucho tiempo" —not long ago, but how long, we do not know. The age of the gentleman is "around fifty," "frisaba... los cincuenta." But most crucially, neither the reader nor the writer is sure of the protagonist's last name:

> Quieren decir que tenía el sobrenombre de Quijada, o Quesada, que en esto hay alguna diferencia en los autores que deste caso escriben; aunque por conjeturas verosímiles se deja entender que se llamaba Quejana. Pero esto importa poco a nuestro cuento; hasta que en la narración del no se salga un punto de la verdad.

> Some say that his surname was Quixada or Quesada (for there is no unanimity among those who write on this subject), although reasonable conjectures tend to show that he was called Quexana. But this scarcely affects our story; it will be enough not to stray a hair's breadth from the truth in telling it.

No one knows how to spell or pronounce correctly the name of the most famous character in fiction. And yet the text is correct when it asserts that this matters little to "our story." The truth of the narration depends on uncertainty and inaccuracy; as soon as "we" human beings start to write and read "our story" to each other, we start to make mistakes and alternate versions of the text. We can only begin to understand each other when we consent to accept that we will be, at least sometimes, misunderstood. And that is one way to understand the problem of origins: these are our best guesses, and we are not sure.

When we read of how Don Quijote names himself, again the problem of multiple and conflicting names appears:

> Puesto nombre, y tan a su gusto, a su caballo, quiso ponersele a si mismo, y en este pensamiento duro otros ocho días, y al cabo se vino a llamar *don Quijote*, de dónde, como queda dicho, tomaron ocasión los autores desta tan verdadera historia que, sin duda, se debía llamar Quijada, y no Quesada, como otros quisieron decir.

> Having got a name for his horse so much to his taste, he was anxious to get one for himself, and he spend eight days more pondering over this point. At last he made up his mind to call himself Don Quijote, —which, as stated above, led the authors of this veracious history to infer that his name quite assuredly must have been Quixada, and not Quesada as others would have it.

Two different ways of writing and reading appear here. One comes from a desire for pleasure; it is a pleasure to name things. Many critics have noted that Don Quijote is a kind of Adam in his dusty Manchegan anti-Eden. He names the crucial elements in his new world. But unlike Adam, who is named by God, he names himself, too, and takes tremendous pleasure—and one day more than God took to create the whole world—in doing it. So he is author of himself, at least for a moment, and there is a tremendous childish pleasure in that, the belief that I am my own author. It avoids dependence on a way of reading and writing that enters into disputation in order unequivocally to establish, not my own name, but the name of the other. Cervantes's historical and cultural moment was one in which lineage was crucial to survival and success. Not to know one's own name was certainly to lose privilege, and possibly to be exposed to caste and class discrimination. As an "hidalgo," Don Quijote belongs to a caste which can trace its origins to "old Christians;" that is, people who have (at least officially) never intermarried with Jews or Muslims. It was a cultural situation in which a slip of a letter or a misspelling could conceivably have had life-or-death consequences. Don Quijote finds a way out of the dilemma by removing himself from the narrative of caste and religious orthodoxy, entering instead the narrative of the outworn chivalric romances, and then carefully renaming himself according to their formula.

Of course, this self-reinscription works only within a very limited sphere, because none of us is our own author. "Quijote" means the piece of armor that covers the thigh. We know that Don Quijote's armor was rusty and broken. Armored writing is the most vulnerable kind. Slavoj Žižek addresses this matter in *The Fragile Absolute.* Here Žižek discusses the practice of John Gray, author of *Men Are from Mars, Women Are from Venus,* itself, interestingly, a courtly love manual. Žižek says that Gray is pseudo-Freudian, in that "Gray accepts the psychoanalytic notion of a hard kernel of some early childhood traumatic experience that forever marked the subject's further development, giving it a pathological turn;"[5] the difficulty is that Gray suggests that the subject should regress to that primal scene, and then rewrite it as non-traumatic and helpful. Žižek continues,

> if, say, your primordial traumatic scene that persisted in your unconscious, distorting and inhibiting your creative attitude, was that of your father shouting at you: 'You're worthless! I despise you! Nothing good will come out of you!', you should rewrite it into a new scene with a benevolent father smiling kindly at you and telling you: 'You're OK! I trust you completely!'[6]

Exercises like this were enacted by Gray and audience members of the *Oprah Winfrey Show.* But Žižek (and Cervantes too) has his doubts. He states them by creating his own absurd revision of one of Freud's most famous case histories, that of the Wolf-Man. This analysis helped Freud to develop several important theories and concepts that have become crucial to the interpretation of narrative. Central to the case of the Wolf-Man is the idea of the primal scene, a crucial, traumatic tableau in which the child sees what he desires to see, but which he is not supposed to see, and which his limited intellectual, emotional, and physical experience makes it impossible for him to understand. Seeing his parents having sex is beyond his interpretive powers, and gives rise to misprisions and conclusions that will have a determining effect on his later life.[7] Žižek returns to the Wolf-Man, whose story is at the beginnings of modern ideas about original trauma, and imagines him following Gray's instructions:

To play this game to the end: when the Wolf-Man "regressed" to the traumatic scene that determined his subsequent psychic development—witnessing the parental *coitus a tergo*—the solution would be to rewrite this scene, so that what the Wolf-Man actually saw was merely his parents lying on the bed, Father reading a newspaper and Mother a sentimental novel.[8]

The problem with Gray's approach, for Žižek, is that it erases not so much "the 'hard facts' but the Real [in the Lacanian sense] of a traumatic encounter whose structuring role in the subject's psychic economy forever resists its symbolic rewriting."[9] The narrative of *Don Quijote*, in both the 1605 and 1615 parts, is the story of a man of La Mancha coming to terms with, and working through, the un-rewritable. Up to a point it is true that nothing is written in stone. But that truism also calls to mind, for example, the Arch of Septimus Severus in Rome. Someone's name was written in stone on that arch, and when the next emperor decided to rewrite a traumatic past, he had to excise those carved letters before inscribing his own. The excision left a scar on the stone of the arch. The new inscription rests on the evidence of the erasure of the old—in other words, rewriting redoubles trauma, and calls attention to its own inefficacy. My attempt at rewriting requires an inescapable allusion to the trauma I wish to negate.

What Cervantes does in *El ingenioso hidalgo Don Quijote de la Mancha* is not to rewrite, but to write for the first time. The narrator's hatred of *libros de caballería* in the Prologue is a hatred of formula, of the kinds of rewriting that pose as originality but which do not take the irreducible trauma of human narration into account. Roland Barthes finds a way to write about this in *The Pleasure of the Text*. He distinguishes between the text of pleasure and the text of bliss (*jouissance*):

> Text of pleasure: the text that contents, fills, grants euphoria; the text that comes from culture and does not break with it, is linked to a *comfortable* practice of reading. Text of bliss: the text that imposes a state of loss, the text that discomforts (perhaps to the point of a certain boredom), unsettles the reader's historical, cultural, psychological assumptions, the consistency of his tastes, values, memories, brings to a crisis his relation with language.[10]

Barthes is aware that it is possible to read two texts—for example, the *Don Quijote* of pleasure and the *Don Quijote* of bliss—simultaneously, but he is also aware that this kind of reading is "doubly perverse," in that I am doing and undoing myself simultaneously in it. By way of Barthes, I could say that formulaic reading and writing put that in me that cannot face difference (either difference from the other or from myself) to sleep. They work like a drug to induce oblivion and stupidity. Teaching "critical reading and writing" practices runs the risk of this kind of deadening formula, in which the rhetoric of critique stands in for feeling, thinking, and writing through traumas of difference and unpredictability.

The book's innovation lies in its relentless narrative exploration of what it is to write something for the first time. To speak of the text as being at the root of modern Western narrative is not inaccurate, but it is to overlook the fact that few writers have been able to do anything like what Cervantes suggests might be necessary in order to work through the life-and-death implications of a culture and literature that depend upon formula. One might even say that what *El ingenioso hidalgo Don Quijote de la Mancha* gives us is an opportunity to see the primal scene of Western narrative, not in order to rewrite it but in order to work it through by reading it unflinchingly for the first time. The argument would be that a liberating discourse is necessarily one the faces the traumatic past and tradition without anesthesia, and then lucidly writes what it sees and cannot see, feels and cannot feel, knows and cannot know.[11]

It is not coincidental that Žižek's ridiculous version of the Wolf-Man's rewrite should have his parents reading in bed. The key to the primal scene of Western narrative is in that version. As an adult, seeing someone else read when you want their attention is not entirely unlike a child seeing his parents having sex when he wants their attention. It can be traumatic to watch someone reading. In the current context, this happens, for example, in the workplace, in which a computer screen with an active email program captivates the person whose attention you are trying to hold or get. This is bad enough face-to-face, but in some ways even worse over the telephone, when you can sense that the other person is reading email silently while you try to converse. It is annoying, to say the least, to sit patiently while someone plows through one email after another in front of you. Don Quijote annoys his family and neighbors because he abandons his social roles and lets his estate fall to ruin so that he can read one chivalric romance after another. His reading becomes traumatic when he begins to live the rhetoric of those stories, and to rewrite his life in accordance with their formulae. The first thing he must rewrite is his horse's name—because there can be no *caballero* without a *caballo*. Once the *caballo*, Rocinante ("the nag before") exists, the *caballero* can come into being, and we have seen some of the process at work when Don Quijote names himself. In order to stabilize the tripod that makes his remade identity possible, then knight needs a Lady, and so must name her:

> Oh, cómo se holgó nuestro buen caballero cuando hubo hecho este discurso, y más cuando halló a quien dar nombre de su dama! Y fue, a lo que se cree, que en un lugar cerca del suyo había una moza labradora de muy buen parecer, de quien él un tiempo anduvo enamorado, aunque, según se entiende, ella jamás lo supo ni se dió cata dello.

> Oh, how our good gentleman enjoyed the delivery of this speech, especially when he had thought of some one to call his lady! There was, so the story goes, in a village near his own a very good-looking farm girl with whom he had at one time

been in love, though, so far as is known, she never knew about it or gave a thought to the matter.

At some time before the narration he had a crush on Aldonza Lorenzo, but she never knew of it. At the time of narration, re-naming this woman who never knew of his love is to escape the difference of her body, and to supplant it with a controllable textual anodyne. The formulaic text, as fetish, replaces the work of relationship with difference. In the nineteenth century, Flaubert gives us Emma Bovary, a tireless reader of sentimental novels, as an example of a simple kind of female quixotism: her choice of reading ruins her life. Žižek's decision to say that the Wolf-Man saw his new, sexless mother reading a sentimental novel is important. After all, he could have said that she was reading a fashion magazine; in fact, that is more parallel with the idea of the father who reads a newspaper. But he says that the mother is reading, specifically, a sentimental novel. Does that mean that she is, like Madame Bovary, an adulteress, who must ultimately be punished? Is that part of the unavoidable kernel of the real, the trace of a trauma that is impossible to erase? Žižek does not escape the formulaic tendencies that Cervantes works so hard to work through.

Like Emma Bovary, Don Quijote dies; unlike her, he does not kill himself. For him, reading takes the place of sexual activity and never gives way to it. But once he stops reading and gets out on the road, Don Quijote begins to encounter female bodies that cannot be controlled or re-named. The first of these, the first people he meets on his first sally, are two prostitutes at the gate of a roadside inn. He addresses them in the language of the romances:

> —No fuyan las vuestras mercedes ni teman desaguisado alguno; ca la orden de caballería que profeso non toca ni atane facerles a ninguno, cuanto mas a tan altas doncellas como vuestras presencias demuestran.

> "Flee not, your ladyships, nor fear ye any harm," he said, "for it belongs not nor pertains to the order of knighthood which I profess to harm anyone, much less highborn maidens as your appearance proclaims you to be." (I, ii)

The prostitutes can barely understand Don Quijote's elaborate rhetoric, but they do understand that he is referring to them as maidens, and they laugh: "mas como se oyeron llamar doncellas, cosa tan fuera de su profesión, no pudieron tener la risa" ("but when they heard themselves called maidens, a thing so much out of their line, they could not restrain their laughter").

So there is no dialogue possible here. From within his fantasy, Don Quijote cannot see sex, and in particular he cannot see sexualized female bodies. Neither prostitutes nor wives are visible to him, which is why at this stage he never considers the fate of Sancho's wife and children. Marriage is entirely outside his rhetorical economy. It literally does not fit. It could be argued that an analysis of marriage is a central theme for Cervantes; irresolvable dilemmas around marriage fill key positions in *Don Quijote*, his *Exemplary Novels* and in other texts. The questions that preoccupied the Council of Trent in its attempts to establish canon law for modern matrimony still concern Cervantes decades later, in his explorations of the meaning of free will, consent, and deception in relation to marriage. Broadly what can be said is that Cervantes questions the degree to which formulae can be applied to any kind of human relationship, and that he explores very thoroughly the degree to which formulae can bring life or death to people and texts. He refuses to romanticize; his explorations of love, literature, and relationships always foreground the impact that rhetoric has on flesh and blood. The one occasion I can recall in which he does lean toward the emotional, although not the sentimental, is in the Prologue to the Second (1615) Part of *Don Quijote*. Here he upbraids his imitator, Alonso Fernández de Avellaneda, for *ad hominem* attacks made in Avellaneda's prologue, in which Avellaneda mocks Cervantes for being old and one-armed:

> Lo que no he podido dejar de sentir es que me note de viejo y de manco, como si hubiera sido en mi mano haber detenido el tiempo, que no pasase por mí. O si mi manquedad hubiera nacido en alguna taberna, sino en la más alta ocasión que vieron los siglos pasados, los presentes, ni esperan ver los venideros.

> What I cannot help resenting is that he charges me with being old and one-handed, as if it had been in my power to hinder time's passage, or as if the loss of my hand had occurred in some tavern and not on the grandest occasion the past or present has seen or the future can hope to see. (Prologue, II)

Please recall that Cervantes lost the use of his left hand as the result of a musket fired at him during the Battle of Lepanto (1571). He had tried, on the basis of his service in this important battle, to gain some kind of pension or preferment from the Crown, and possibly even a post in the New World. But nothing came from his efforts. His rhetoric is strong, as it is elsewhere in the Second Part. Mortality is a concern here, in a way that it is not in the First Part from ten years earlier. By the end of the Second Part, the reader has witnessed, without a doubt, the death of Don Quijote. Cervantes himself dies in 1616. Both the First and Second Parts take the body, whatever its gender or degree of sexual expression, extremely seriously, and teach that although violence can sometimes look very funny, it never is when it is happening to you. Cervantes's wounded and disabled hand marks the point where the body, the read, and the written meet. His unsought wound helps to explain a text in which male virgins, old married men, prostitutes, aristocratic wives, lost lovers of any and all genders can meet each other and interrupt each other's expectations. In itself this is a great innovation. But Cervantes goes further. Instead of trying to contain or rewrite difference, sexual or otherwise, he risks a narrative strategy that few if any, before or after him, have attempted. There is marriage and heartbreak, violence and disappointment in *El ingenioso hidalgo Don Quijote de la Mancha*.

The trajectory of Western narrative is filled with women, dead or dying, upon whose death the whole of narrative depends. But Cervantes, perhaps because he knows what killing is, because he knows what war is, does not participate in the carnage.

Don Quijote does not depend on dead female or feminized bodies. The female body may scare him, it is true, so he armors himself before he goes out on his first sally—but his shabby, rusty, broken armor is itself traumatized. His greatest triumph—perhaps his only triumph—is that he leaves home and goes out on the road unprotected. He has faith that the chivalric vocabulary will uphold him, but that rhetoric is shortly seen to be as rickety as his horse. If he wishes to be a *caballero andante*, a knight errant—that is, if he wishes to wander, to err—he has to give up the hermetic seal of chivalric discourse. This does not happen until after his first sally, when the priest, the barber, and the women of his house deprive him of his chivalric cookbooks. When he goes out a second time, without access to them, he becomes susceptible to dialogue. This entry into dialogue happens first with Sancho Panza. He promises Sancho a governorship, and that hope of something different is enough justification for Sancho to go along for the ride. But crucially, Don Quijote does not rename Sancho. Sancho's is the first difference that Don Quijote can confront on its own terms. It is an unyielding difference that permeates even Sancho's language; his malapropisms make it impossible for Don Quijote to insert Sancho into the purity of his orthodox chivalric rhetoric. Because he is able to face Sancho's difference, slowly, over hundreds of pages, in a narrative process that makes psychoanalysis look fast and easy, Don Quijote can gradually face the trauma of otherness in what has historically been, in the West, its most graphic form; that is, the trauma of sexual difference. Don Quijote can begin to discover difference in dialogue with another man, in a situation in which the differences and likenesses do not disrupt the flow of his inquiry. I do not think that Don Quijote's and Sancho's relationship is homoerotic; I do not think it is even homosocial. In fact, I do not think it is homo- anything, insofar as the prefix "homo-" means "the same." For what it is worth, I would not be willing to argue for anybody's heterosexuality in this context either, in that the "hetero-" (different) of heterosexuality in today's rhetoric of sexuality could not more emphatically mean "the Same," with a capital S.

The concept of "same difference," perhaps the dominant formula in global capitalism and its social formations, is the subject of *S/Z*, another of Roland Barthes' crucial works. Here Barthes does a microscopically close reading of Balzac's short story, "Sarrasine." In terms of sexual difference and the problem of the Same, what is important about "Sarrasine" is that, at least according to conventional French onomastics, it is misspelled. The name should be spelled with a "z" instead of with a second "s." The story tells of a powerful man, Sarrasine, who falls in love with La Zambinella, having believed that La Zambinella is a woman, and then of the traumatic effects of his discovery, or admittal, that La Zambinella is certainly feminized, but not a woman, and not a man, either. La Zambinella is, in fact, the name that a beautiful castrato assumes. For Barthes, the strange use of the letter S where the letter Z should be is the mark of cutting and difference in the text. The un-rewritable trace of its crucial trauma, which is linked to sexuality and sexual difference, is ever before the reader, right in the middle of the title and professional name of the text's key character. Z reverses S, breaking its curves into pointy shards. Barthes' study, the fruit of a term-long seminar at the Collège de France, gives emphatic evidence of the difference one little letter can make.

Balzac, of course, was not the first author to make literature of this observation. Cervantes knows what a difference a letter can make, too. All of the names of our hero have something in common, and that is the letter Q. If you are still willing, find something to write with and something to write on and slowly begin to write the letter Q. Do it more than once. Try to recall writing the letter Q when you were just learning how to write. Think of the block letter Q, and the strange cursive Q, and its unusual variants. What makes the letter Q so queer? Why is it so much fun to write it? Or perhaps it is not fun to write it at all. Maybe it is too difficult. Why do we use Q, anyway? Who needs it?

Sebastián de Covarrubias tries to explain this in his 1611 dictionary, *Tesoro de la lengua castellana*:[12]

> la razón de usar della es porque siguiéndole siempre la U ayunte en una sílaba la vocal siguiente. Vide Quintilianum, lib. 12, cap. 10: "Apud latinos saepe Q mutatur in C, ut loquor, locutus, sequor, secutus."

> (the reason for using it is that it being always followed by U it joins into one syllable with the following vowel. See Quintilian, book 12, chapter 10, "according to the Latin speakers, the q often changes to a c, so loquor, locutus, sequor, secutus" [I speak, having spoken; I follow, having followed].[13]

One reason for using Q, even though K and C can sometimes seem sufficient, is that Q and U go together and work a kind of magic over any vowel they run across. For all its eccentricity, Q needs U more than any other consonant needs any other vowel. Q does not make any sense without U. Some of this understanding of Q becomes clear from the practice of writing the letter. First, make a circle. Don Quijote leaves his home in La Mancha at the beginning of the First Part, and over a thousand pages and ten years later he returns to die, finishing at his starting point. The narrative starts and ends at home in La Mancha. It is like the great circle we must draw in order to make the letter "Q." So the initial movements required in writing Q track Don Quijote's movements. But then, in order to distinguish Q from O, the writer has to do something unforeseen, which is to mar the perfection of that great O. To write Q you have to break the circle with a line. The circuit must be interrupted or what is written is just another O. That mark is a blow, the sign of trauma. It is what makes Q different from O. It is something extra, an excessive mark that interrupts the clarity of the circle. The little line is the mark of difference itself. The little line that crosses over the circle interrupts the circuit of repetition. A wished-for wholeness and unity and seamlessness must be interrupted if I wish to write "Q." I have to mar the repeatable in order to be able to write that which needs U in order mean anything.

Of course the pun does not work in Spanish in the same way that it does in English. In English, the point is that *El ingenioso hidalgo Don Quijote de la Mancha* shows the reader that without U, Q is nothing (a big zero)—and that without Q there will be all kinds of important things that U will never be able to say. In Spanish, Q needs U, too, and vice-versa. "U" is one way to say "or" in Spanish. Not surprisingly, the other way is "O." "U" is used instead of "o" before words that begin with "o" or "ho." To the extent that Q in English always pronounces the second person (you), Q in Spanish is always saying "u," other. In both cases, the letter is unusual in that it insists on a relationship. It relies on its own brokenness in order to make sense. It is not a matter of repetition; in fact, it is an insistence that the rote is no way to go.

Sancho personifies the rupture with the rote. He constantly interrupts Don Quijote, most regularly when Don Quijote is spinning off down a vortex of chivalric rhetoric. Don Quijote hates having his monologues interrupted, and upbraids Sancho. But as the two travel along the road together, and begin to experience events together, Don Quijote's chivalric monologues diminish, and dialogues begin to develop between the two men. A conversation opens up, and love blooms. But it is not romantic or chivalric love, or even the love of friendship. What blossoms as Don Quijote and Sancho move along the road together, never knowing what is going to happen next, is charity. The hermetic, formulaic rhetoric of dead chivalry breaks open to reveal what makes charity possible. Sancho is possibly the first practitioner of what Neil Wilson, W.V. Quine, and Donald Davidson have called "the Principle of Charity."[14] Davidson explores the ways in which people can use language to understand each other; to explain the Principle of Charity he says:

> the fact that a theory does not make speakers universal holders of truths is not an inadequacy of the theory; the aim is not the absurd one of making disagreement and error disappear. The point is rather that widespread agreement is the only possible background against which disputes and mistakes can be interpreted. Making sense of the utterances and behaviour of others, even their most aberrant behaviour, requires us to find a great deal of reason and truth in them. To see too much unreason on the part of others is simply to undermine our ability to understand what it is they are so unreasonable about.[15]

That last sentence summarizes the position of the women of Don Quijote's household, and that of his friends, in relation to his literary madness. To call someone crazy can be a way to shut down any possibility for dialogue with them, to eradicate relationship with them. To reiterate, the principle of charity is the idea "that widespread agreement is the only possible background against which disputes and mistakes can be interpreted." The "purpose is to make meaningful disagreement possible, and this depends entirely on a foundation—*some* foundation—in agreement."[16] Finally, "Charity is forced on us; whether we like it or not, if we want to understand others, we must count them right in most matters."[17] Before he met Sancho, everyone he knew counted Don Quijote wrong on all matters. But Sancho is able to practice the principle of charity—colloquially, he agrees to disagree with Don Quijote. He finds a tiny space for agreement, an excuse for agreement, in the form of the promise of the governorship, and then spends many succeeding chapters meaningfully disagreeing with Don Quijote. As a result, love, in this charitable sense, develops between the two men.

It is important to note that Davidson introduces a condition in his explanation of the principle of charity. The key phrase in that sentence is, "if we want to understand others." So a desire to understand others on their own terms, which I think must be connected to a wish to be understood oneself, is the precondition for meaningful agreement and disagreement. This is not a desire to convert, compel, or convince the other. This form of understanding is closest to the activity of bearing witness to and with the other. And this can be done only from a position of radical undefendedness, or what Shoshona Felman calls (after Paul Celan), "shelterlessness," in which one "gives reality one's own vulnerability, as a condition of exceptional availability and of exceptionally sensitized, tuned in attention to the *relation between language and events*."[18] He may interrupt a lot, but Sancho is a great listener. He knows how to stand by Don Quijote, how to come back after he flees, how to take his own beatings, and how to salve Don Quijote's wounds. And then he knows how to enter into conversation about all of it.

"If we want to understand others," we have to see first that we cannot even spell our own names, not because we do not care, but because we have so many. We need each other to help us each understand our many names. Books alone cannot accomplish this. Books are great but their greatness is only revealed when you have someone with whom to talk about them. This other does not even have to have read the book. The other does not have to agree with your reading. The other just has to want to understand you. Of course, there are some things you cannot say, and that is what writing is for. Literature is a special kind of writing. Barbara Johnson says, "Literature [...] is not to be understood as a predetermined set of works but as a mode of cultural work, the work of giving-to-read those impossible contradictions that cannot yet be spoken."[19] When we put pen to paper and write Q, we are near the root of literature. The hand and the pen make strange twists and turns as they write Q. The ink never breaks into the circle at the same place twice, no matter how many times you have written the letter. The eye, reading Q, makes an effort to distinguish it from O, and then looks for U.

You can go to La Mancha and find many businesses engaged in selling tourist maps that trace out "La ruta de Don Quijote," "The Route of Don Quijote." People try to follow it, but they cannot, because there are stretches in the book in which Don Quijote is missing in action; it is not possible to follow in his footsteps, because nobody knows where he went. If you add a U to "rote" you get "route," but I am not going to tell you where you will end up.

Notes

1   Grateful acknowledgement is made to Macalester College, for whose International Roundtable on *Don Quijote* this chapter was originally commissioned.

2   Miguel de Cervantes, *El ingenioso hidalgo Don Quijote de la Mancha*, ed. John Jay Allen (Madrid: Ediciones Cátedra, 1994). Some people have strong preferences about editions and translations of *Don Quijote*, and of course there are very many available. I have used the Norton critical edition, ed. Jones and Douglas. I have cited the text by Part and Chapter rather than by page number.

3   de Lauretis, "Desire in Narrative," 156.

4   Genesis itself provides two narratives for the origin of the world, so in fact the canonical text of origins eludes the desire for a unitary narrative, too.

5   Žižek, *The Fragile Absolute*, 107–08.

6   Ibid., 108.

7   "Primal Scene [:] Scene of sexual intercourse between the parents which the child observes, or infers on the basis of certain indications, and phantasises. It is generally interpreted by the child as an act of violence on the part of the father." J. Laplanche and J.-B. Pontalis. *The Language of Psycho-Analysis*, trans. Donald Nicholson-Smith (New York: W. W. Norton, 1973), 335.

8   Žižek, *The Fragile Absolute*, 108.

9   Ibid., 109.

10 Roland Barthes, *The Pleasure of the Text*, trans. Richard Miller (New York: Hill and Wang, 1975), 14.

11 Toni Morrison's *Beloved* is an example of a novel that does this uncompromising work.

12 Sebastian de Covarrubias y Orozco, *Tesoro de la lengua*, Madrid 1611, 843.

13 Professor Sarolta Takacs (Classics, Rutgers University) kindly provided the Latin translation and searched for the citation from Quintilian. Covarrubias may have used a corrupt text; a thorough search of databases could not find this quotation.

14 Donald Davidson, *Inquiries into Truth and Interpretation* (Oxford: Oxford University Press, 2nd ed., 2001). Davidson explains the development and meaning of the principle of charity throughout the essays in this collection.

15 Ibid., 153.

16 Ibid., 196–97.

17 Ibid., 197.

18 Shoshona Felman in Shoshona Felman and Dori Laub, M. D., *Testimony: Crises of Witnessing in Literature, Psychoanalysis, and History* (New York: Routledge, 1992).

19 Johnson, *The Feminist Difference*, 13.

Bibliography

Abraham, Nicholas, and Torok, Maria. *The Wolf-Man's Magic Word: A Cryptonomy*. Trans. Nicholas Rand. Minneapolis, MN: University of Minneapolis Press, 1986.

The American Heritage Dictionary. Boston: Houghton Mifflin, 4th edn, 2000.

Attridge, Derek, ed. *The Cambridge Companion to James Joyce*. Cambridge: Cambridge University Press, 1990.

——. *Joyce Effects: On Language, Theory and History*. Cambridge: Cambridge University Press, 2000.

Avellaneda, Alonso Fernández de. *The Second Volume of the Ingenious Gentleman Don Quijote of la Mancha* (1614).

Barthes, Roland. *S/Z*. Trans. Richard Miller. New York: Hill and Wang, 1974.

Bartlett, John. *Familiar Quotations*. Gen. ed. Justin Kaplan. Boston: Little, Brown, 16th edn 1992.

Bonaparte, Marie. "The Murders in Rue Morgue," *Psychoanalytic Quarterly* 4 (1935): 259–93.

Brooks, Peter. "Fictions of the Wolf-Man: Freud and Narrative Understanding" [1982], *Reading for the Plot: Design and Intention in Narrative*. Cambridge, MA: Harvard University Press, 1994, 264–85.

Bridgman, Richard. *Gertrude Stein in Pieces*. New York: Oxford University Press, 1970.

Butler, Christopher. "Joyce, Modernism, and Post-modernism," *The Cambridge Companion to James Joyce*. Ed. Derek Attridge. Cambridge: Cambridge University Press, 1990, 259–82.

Butler, Judith. "Variations on Sex and Gender: Beauvoir, Wittig and Foucault," *Feminism as Critique: Essays on the Politics of Gender in Late-Capitalist Societies*. Ed. Seyla Benhabib and Drucilla Cornell. Cambridge: Polity Press, 1987, 128–42.

Cervantes, Miguel de. *The Ingenious Gentleman Don Quijote of La Mancha*, Parts I and II, *Don Quijote: A Norton Critical Edition*. Ed. Joseph R. Jones and Kenneth Douglas. New York: W. W. Norton, 1981.

—— *Coloquio de los perros. Novelas ejemplares*. Vol. 3. Ed. Juan Bautista Avalle-Arce. Madrid: Castalia, 1985.

Chaucer, Geoffrey. *Romaunt of the Rose, Romaunt of the Rose [and] Minor Poems, The Complete Works*. Vol. 1. Ed. Walter W. Skeat. Oxford: Clarendon Press, 1894.

Chilton, John. *Billie's Blues: Billie Holiday's Story, 1933–1959*. New York: Stein & Day, 1975.

Clarke, Donald. *Wishing on the Moon: The Life and Times of Billie Holiday*. New York: Viking, 1994.

Conan Doyle, A. *A Study in Scarlet* [1887], *The Complete Sherlock Holmes*. Vol. I. New York: Doubleday, 1922, 15–86.

Cullingford, Elizabeth Butler. "Phoenician Genealogies and Oriental Geographies: Joyce, Language and Race," *Semicolonial Joyce*. Ed. Derek Attridge and Marjorie Howes. Cambridge: Cambridge University Press, 2000, 219–39.

d'Orleans, Charles. "Rondeaux 54," *Ballades et rondeaux*. Paris: Librarie générale française, 1992.

de Lauretis, Teresa. "Desire in Narrative," *Alice Doesn't: Feminism, Semiotics, Cinema*. London: Macmillan, 1984, 103–57.

——. "Eccentric Subjects: Feminist Theory and Historical Consciousness," *Feminist Studies* 16.1 (Spring 1990): 115–50.

de Lorris, Guillaume. *Le Roman de la Rose*. Vol. I. Paris: Librairie Honoré Champion Éditeur, 1983.

du Bois, Page. "A Disturbance of Syntax at the Gates of Rome," *Stanford Literature Review* 2.2. (Fall 1985): 185–208.

Durán, Manuel. "Cervantes' Harassed and Vagabond Life," *Don Quijote: A Norton Critical Edition*. Ed. Joseph R. Jones and Kenneth Douglas. New York: W. W. Norton, 1981, 833–41.

Elliot, J. H. *Imperial Spain, 1469–1716*. New York: St. Martin's Press, 1963.

Engelbrecht, Penelope J. "'Lifting Belly Is a Language': The Postmodern Lesbian Subject," *Feminist Studies* 16.1 (Spring 1990): 85–114.

Ezzat, Dina. "Islamic Law Drives Arab Women to Illegal Surgery to Save their Lives," *The Times* (London), June 16, 1996.

Findlay, Heather. "Is there a Lesbian in this Text? Derrida, Wittig, and the Politics of the Three Women," *Coming to Terms: Feminism, Theory, Politics*. Ed. Elizabeth Weed. New York: Routledge, 1989, 59–69.

Fish, Stanley. "Withholding the Missing Portion: Power, Meaning and Persuasion in Freud's *The Wolf Man*," *The Linguistics of Writing: Arguments Between Language and Literature*. Ed. Derek Attridge, Alan Durant, Nigel Fabb and Colin MacCabe. Manchester: Manchester University Press, 1987, 155–72.

Freud, Sigmund. *Civilization and Its Discontents* (1930 [1929]), *The Standard Edition of the Complete Works of Sigmund Freud*. Vol. 21. Ed. and trans. James Strachey. London: The Hogarth Press, 1961, 59–148.

——. "A Disturbance of Memory on the Acropolis" [1937], *The Standard Edition of the Complete Works of Sigmund Freud*. Vol. 22. Ed. and trans. James Strachey. London: The Hogarth Press, 1963, 239–48.

—— "From the History of an Infantile Neurosis," *The Standard Edition of the Complete Works of Sigmund Freud*. Vol. 17. Ed. and trans. James Strachey. London: The Hogarth Press, 1953, 7–122.

——. "Screen Memories" [1899], *The Standard Edition of the Complete Works of Sigmund Freud*. Vol. 3. Ed. and trans. James Strachey. London: The Hogarth Press, 1953, 301–22.

——. "The Uncanny" [1919], *The Standard Edition of the Complete Works of Sigmund Freud.* Vol. 17. Ed. and trans. James Strachey. London: The Hogarth Press, 1953, 217–52.

Gardiner, Muriel, ed. *The Wolf-Man,* by the Wolf-Man, with *The Case of the Wolf-Man,* by Sigmund Freud and *A Supplement,* by Anna Freud. New York: Hill and Wang (The Noonday Press), 1991.

Gay, Peter. *Freud: A Life for Our Time.* New York: W. W. Norton, 1988.

Gibbon, Edward. *The Decline and Fall of the Roman Empire* [1787]. 3 Vols. Ed. Oliphant Smeaton. New York: The Modern Library (Random House), 1954(?).

Gilman. Stephen. "The Apocryphal Quijote," *Don Quijote: A Norton Critical Edition.* Ed. Joseph R. Jones and Kenneth Douglas. New York: W. W. Norton, 1981, 994–1002.

Gilmore, Leigh. "An Anatomy of Absence: Written on the Body, The Lesbian Body and Autobiography Without Names," *The Gay 90s: Disciplinary and Interdisciplinary Formations in Queer Studies.* Ed. Thomas Foster, Carol Siegel, and Ellen E. Berry. New York: New York University Press, 1997, PP?.

González-Echevarría, Roberto. *Celestina's Brood: Continuities of the Baroque in Spanish and Latin American Literature.* Durham, NC: Duke University Press, 1993.

Gossy, Mary. *The Untold Story: Women and Theory in Golden Age Texts.* Ann Arbor, MI: University of Michigan Press, 1989.

Hardwick, Michael. *The Sherlock Holmes Companion.* New York: Doubleday, 1963.

Holbrook, Susan. "Lifting Bellies, Filling Petunias, and Making Meaning through the Trans-Poetic," *American Literature* 71.4 (1999): 751–71.

Iser, Wolfgang. *The Act of Reading: A Theory of Aesthetic Response.* Baltimore, MD: Johns Hopkins University Press, 1978.

Johnson, Barbara. "Introduction," *The Feminist Difference: Literature, Psychoanalysis, Race, and Gender.* Cambridge, MA: Harvard University Press, 1998, 1–15.

——. "'Aesthetic' and 'Rapport' in Toni Morrison's *Sula," The Feminist Difference: Literature, Psychoanalysis, Race, and Gender.* Cambridge, MA: Harvard University Press, 1998, 74–87.

Joyce, James. *Ulysses.* Ed. Hans Walter Gabler. New York: Random House, 1986.

Kandela, Peter. "Egypt's Trade in Hymen Repair," *The Lancet* 347 (June 8, 1996): 1615.

Kauffman, L.A. "220,000 Jesus Fans Can't Be Wrong: Praise the Lord, and Mammon," *The Nation* 259/9 (September 25, 1994): 306–10.

Logmans, A., Verhoeff, A., Bol Raap, R., Creighton, F., and M. van Lent, M. "Ethical Dilemma: Should Doctors Reconstruct the Vaginal State," *British Medical Journal* 316 (February 7, 1998): 459–60.

McKitterick, Rosamond, and Quinault, Roland, eds. *Edward Gibbon and Empire.* Cambridge: Cambridge University Press, 1997.

"More Chinese Women Seek to Regain Virginity," *Deutsche Presse-Agentur,* December 14, 1994.

Nebrija, Antonio de. *Gramática de la lengua castellana.* Madrid: Ediciones de Cultura Hispánica, 1992.

Owens, David M. "Gertrude Stein's 'Lifting Belly' and The Great War," *Modern Fiction Studies* 44.3 (1998): 608–18.

Poe, Edgar Allan. *The Murders in the Rue Morgue: Tales of Mystery and Imagination*. London: J. M. Dent, 1912, 378–410.

——. *The Pit and the Pendulum. The Works of Edgar Allan Poe*. Vol. II. New York: P. F. Collier & Sons, 1904, 378–410.

Quartermain, Peter. *Disjunctive Poetics: From Gertrude Stein and Louis Zukofsky to Susan Howe*. Cambridge: Cambridge University Press, 1992.

Robertson, John. "Gibbon's Roman Empire as a Universal Monarchy: The Decline and Fall and the Imperial Idea in Early Modern Europe," *Edward Gibbon and Empire*. Ed. Rosamond McKitterick and Roland Quinault. Cambridge: Cambridge University Press, 1997, 247–70.

Rojas, Fernando de. *La Celestina; tragicomedia de Calisto y Melibea*. Ed. Dorothy S. Severin. Madrid: Alianza Editorial, 1969.

Silverman, Kenneth. *Edgar A. Poe: Mournful and Never-ending Remembrance*. New York: HarperCollins, 1991.

Stearns, David Patrick. "Long, Long Opera, Fallible Characters Demand Attention," *USA Today*, July 13, 1999, sec. 4D.

Stein, Gertrude. *The Autobiography of Alice B. Toklas, Selected Writings of Gertrude Stein*. Ed. Carl Van Vechten. New York: Vintage Books, 1990, 1–238.

——. "Four Saints in Three Acts," *Selected Writings of Gertrude Stein*. Ed. Carl Van Vechten. New York: Vintage Books, 1990, 577–613.

——. "Lifting Belly," *The Yale Gertrude Stein*. Selections by Richard Kostelanetz. New Haven, CT: Yale University Press, 1980, 4–54.

White, John. *Billie Holiday: Her Life and Times*. New York: Universe Books, 1987.

Wittig, Monique. *Les Guérillères*. Paris: Éditions de Minuit, 1969.

——. *The Lesbian Body*. Trans. David Le Vay. Boston: Beacon Press, 1975.

——. "The Straight Mind," *The Straight Mind and Other Essays*. Boston: Beacon Press, 1992.

——, and Zeig, Sande. *Lesbian Peoples: Material for a Dictionary*. New York: Avon, 1979.

Zimic, Stanislav. "El casamiento engañoso y Coloquio de los perros," *Boletín de la Biblioteca de Menéndez Pelayo* 70 (1994): 55–125.

Žižek, Slavoj. *The Fragile Absolute: Or, Why is the Christian Legacy Worth Fighting For?* New York: Verso, 2000.

——. *The Sublime Object of Ideology*. London: Verso, 1989.

Index